Time for HOMEWORK

Paul
Nightingale

K

Kindergarten

Hunter
Education
Nightingale

HUNTER
EDUCATION
NIGHTINGALE

Time for Homework - Kindergarten

Published by:
Hunter Education Nightingale
ABN: 69 055 798 626
PO Box 547
Warners Bay NSW 2282
Ph: 0417 658 777
email: sales@huntereducationnightingale.com.au
paul@huntereducationnightingale.com.au
www.huntereducationnightingale.com.au

Cover Design: Doriana Berkovic

National Library of Australia Card No.
and ISBN 978 - 1 - 922242 - 24 - 2

RECYCLING

When the program is completed and the paper no longer wanted, be sure to have it recycled.
The time and care taken to recycle may help save a tree and maintain our environment.

Time for Homework
Kindergarten/Foundation

Time for Homework Kindergarten is the first in a series of seven books written to help reinforce many of the concepts, skills and understanding needed with today's school curriculum. The series is designed as a user friendly resource that treats reading, handwriting, spelling, grammar, writing and mathematics.

The book contains 30 units of work. Each unit can be attempted over the period of one week. Each unit addresses words and sounds, with an emphasis on identifying and colouring to develop fine motor skills essential for good handwriting. The units also treat topics addressed in today's environment and those in the new Australian Curriculum for Mathematics and English.

As the child's skills develop with sounds and words, the book introduces stories and rhymes. Rhymes are key learning techniques that are catchy to the ear of the child. They help in the development of word families too. In addition the child is introduced to comprehension, punctuation and some grammar. At all times there is an emphasis on spelling and word association.

While *Time for Homework* treats many of the topics presented in the school curriculum, it is a summary of those subjects. This book is fun to use at home for the child in the first year of school. *Time for Homework* is a resource that will help develop learning.

Message to Parents

Time for Homework Kindergarten will need you to help with reading instructions. As a parent you are asked to help with this skill, but please resist the temptation to actually provide answers. Help with explanation, where necessary and assist when needed. As your child works through the book your help will be required less. Reading, maths, handwriting and spelling skills will develop allowing the child to become a more independent learner with an understanding of the topics treated.

Regular homework helps develop skills in the subject areas treated and confidence in your child with learning which is essential for a good education.

Praise your child at all times, because you are the ideal support person in your child's life. Working together will help with the use of this book. It will help make the learning process more meaningful for you both. *Time for Homework Kindergarten* is designed as a fun book to use at home. Enjoy the journey!

 Colour the objects starting with the letter **b**.

b

bus

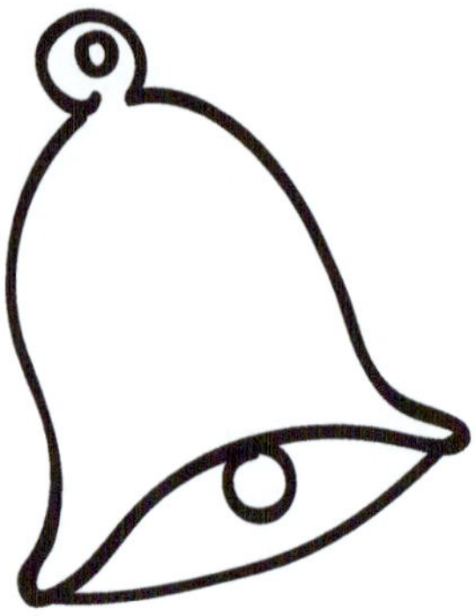

bell

tin

boy

cat

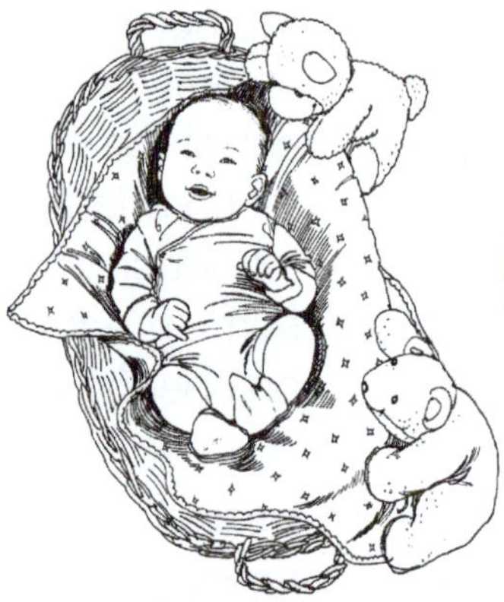

baby

book

Handwriting

Trace the downstrokes.

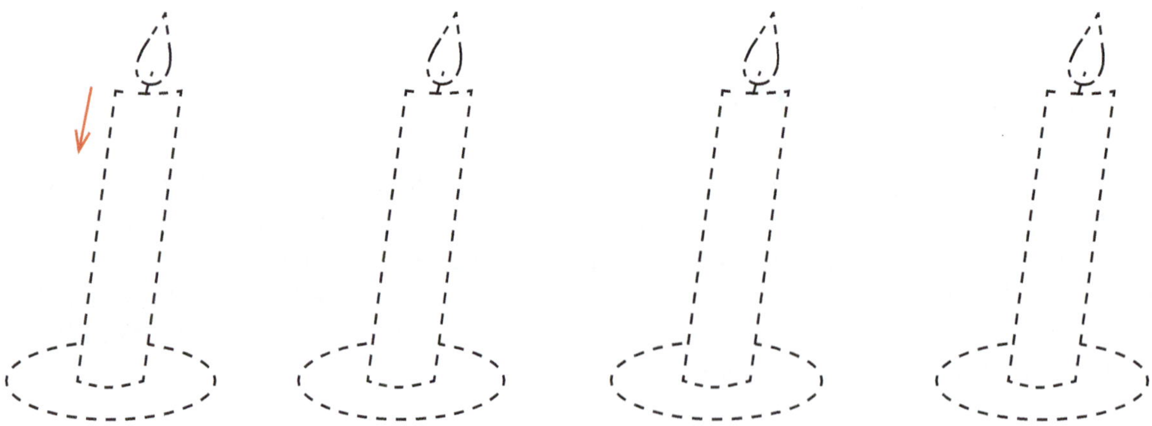

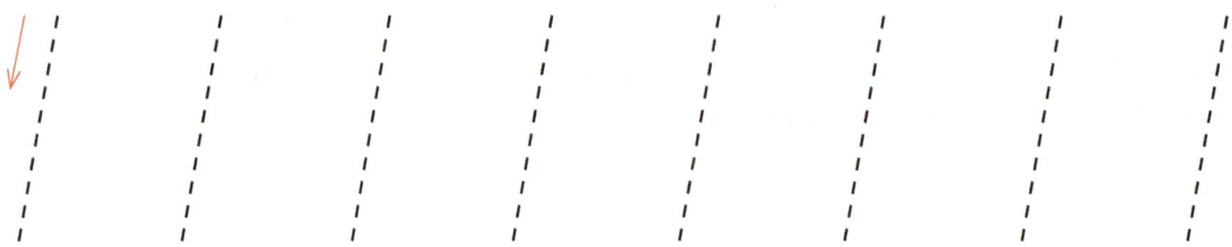

Match the pictures and words.

bell

boy

bus

baby

book

Maths

Colour **one** balloon.

Trace over **one** and number **1**.

one 1 1 1 1

Colour the pictures that start with the letter **m**.

m

man

monkey

milk

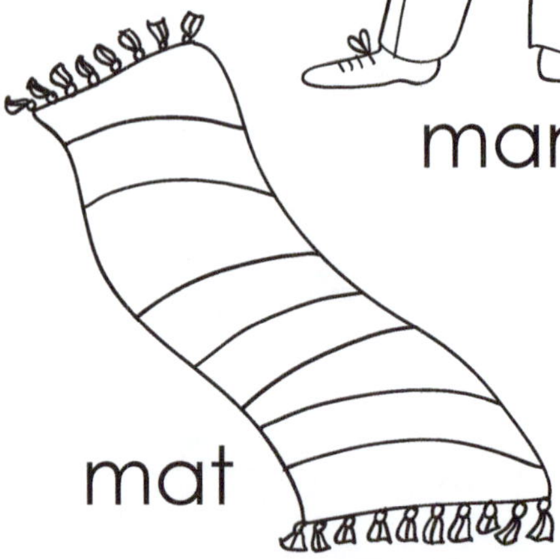

mat

mum

dog

Handwriting

Trace the snail shells.

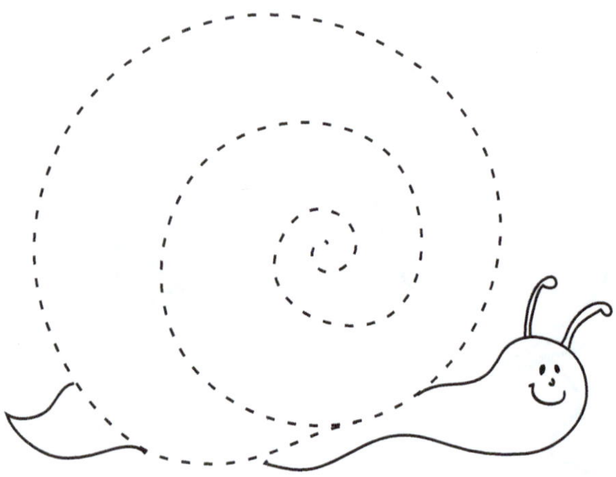

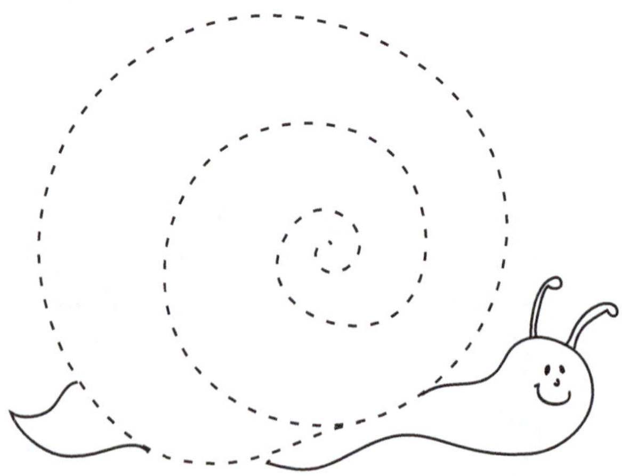

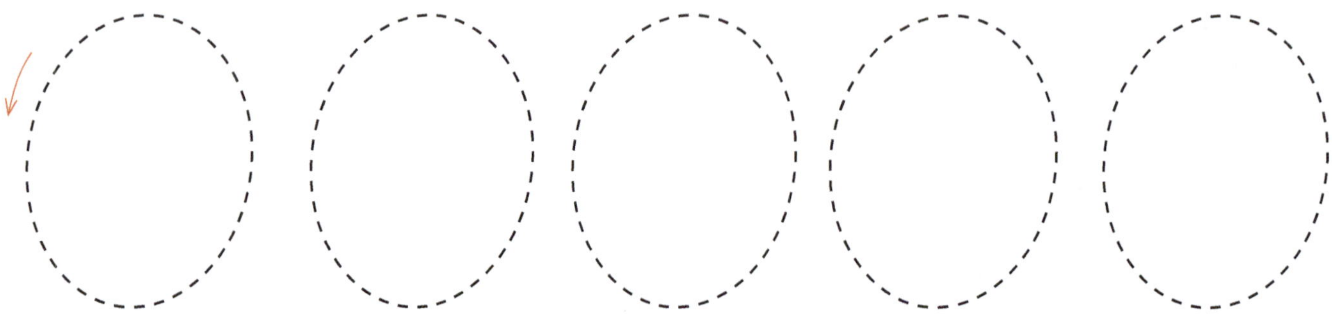

Match the pictures and words.

mum

monkey

mouse

man

milk

mat

Colour **two** cup cakes.

Trace over **two** and number **2**.

two 2 2 2 2

Colour the pictures that start with the letter **t**.

t

tin

apple

tap

tea pot

tie

bike

television

tiger

Handwriting

Trace the elephants.

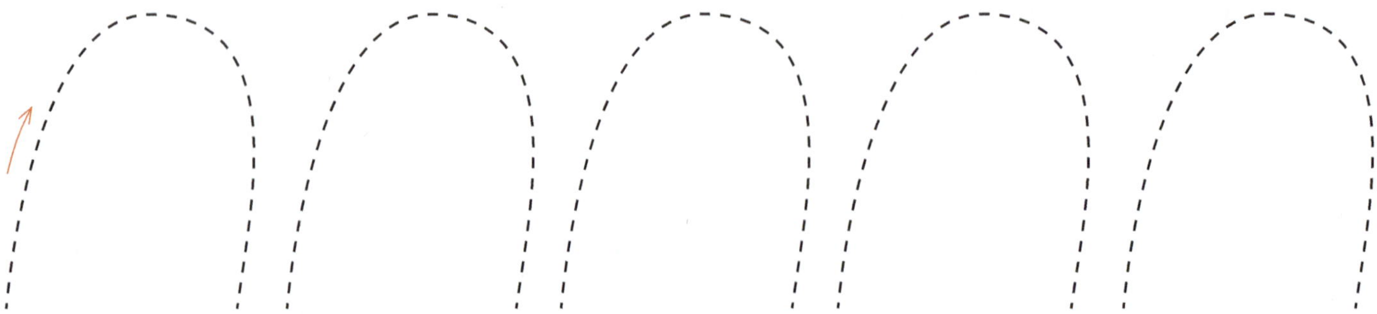

Match the words and pictures.

tin

tap

television

tie

tiger

teapot

Maths

Colour the **longer** snake and the **longest** pencil.

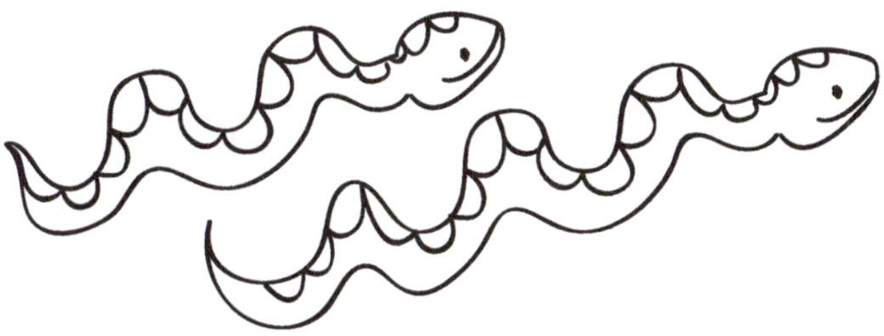

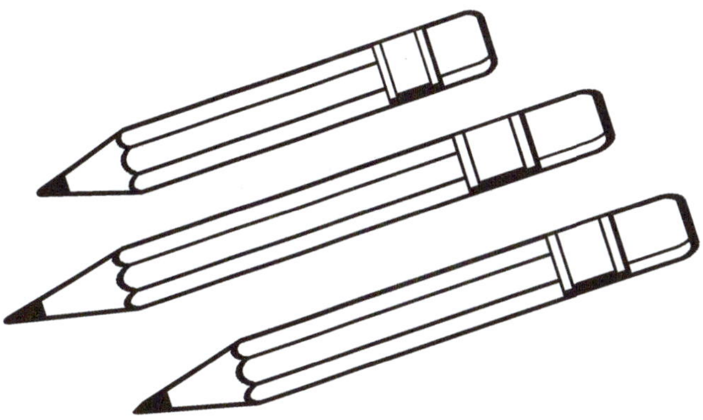

Colour the **heaviest** one.

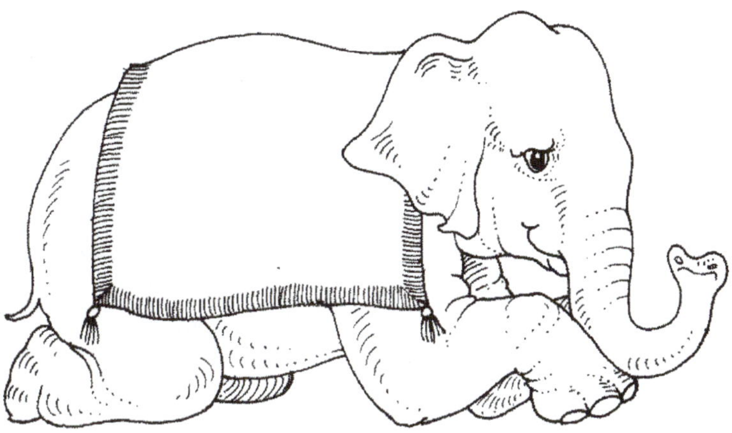

 Colour the pictures that start with the letter **s**.

s

scissors

duck

snail

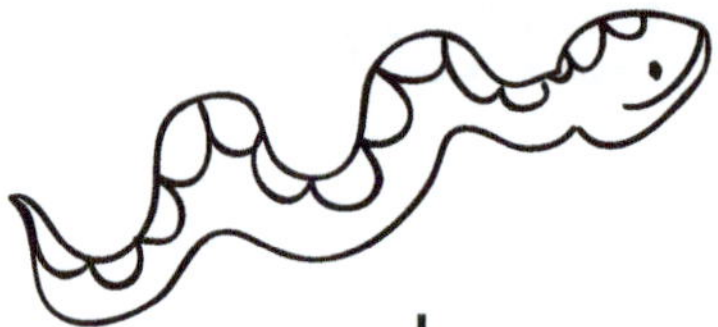

snake

elephant

six

soap

shirt

Handwriting

Trace over each letter.

lamp

igloo

Match the words and pictures.

snail

soap

scissors

shirt

six

snake

Maths

Trace the numbers then match each one to its name.

1 2 3 4

two four one three

Colour **four** balls.

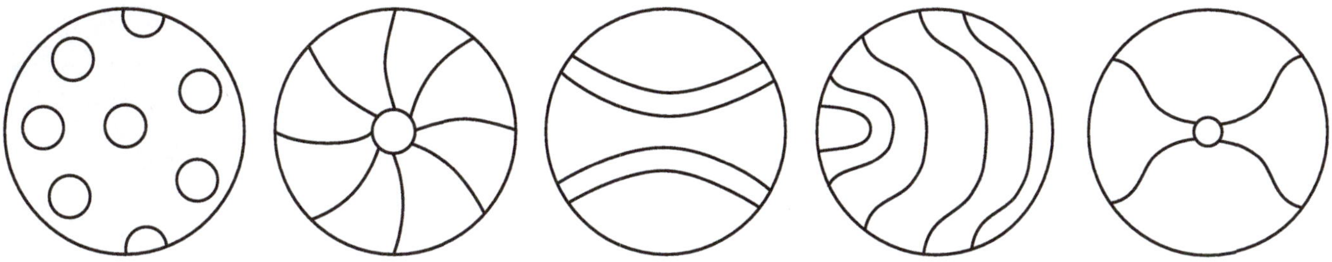

Colour the pictures that start with the letter **c**.

c

car

girl

cow

cot

candle

cup

shirt

cat

Handwriting

Trace over each letter.

t t t t t t

tiger

n n n n n

net

Match the words to the pictures. Read them.

car

cat

candle

cup

cow

cot

Maths

Tick the **full** bottle.

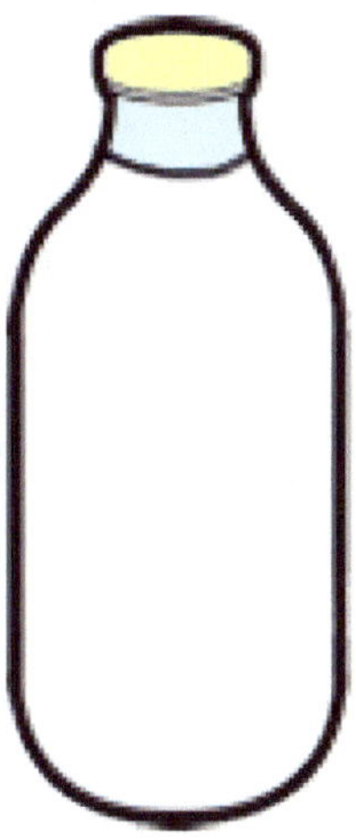

Colour the one that **does not** belong.

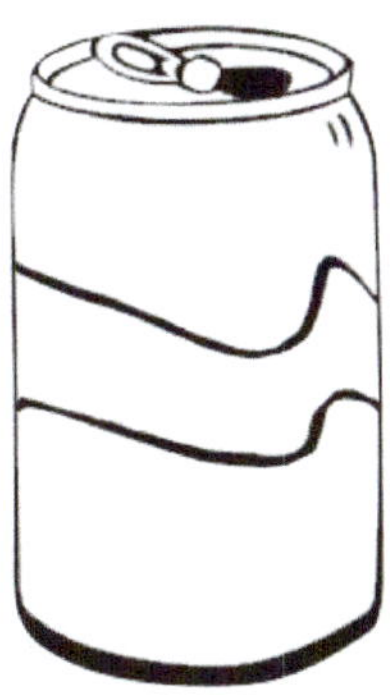

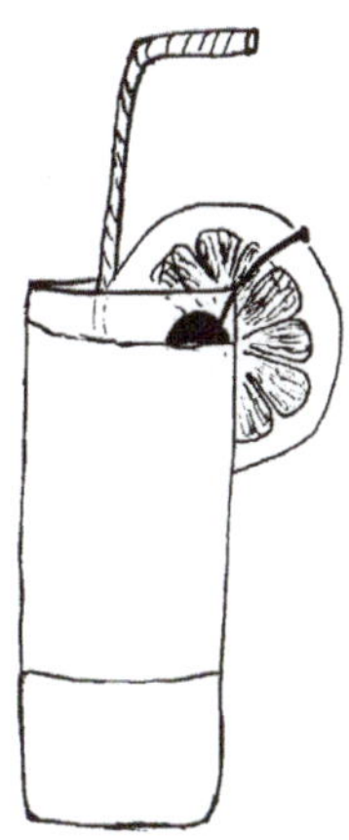

Colour the pictures that start with the letter **d**.

d

drum

dog

doll

door

duck

dress

cat

orange

Handwriting

Trace over each letter.

m m m m

h h h h h

r r r r r

man

hat

rat

Match the words with the pictures.
Read the words.

dog

drum

dress

doll

duck

door

Maths

Colour the shapes that are the **same** in each group.

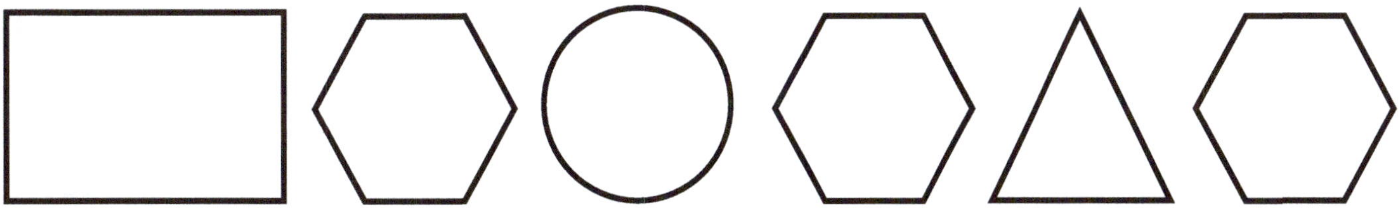

Colour the pictures that start with the letter **h**.

h

house

hat

hammer

girl

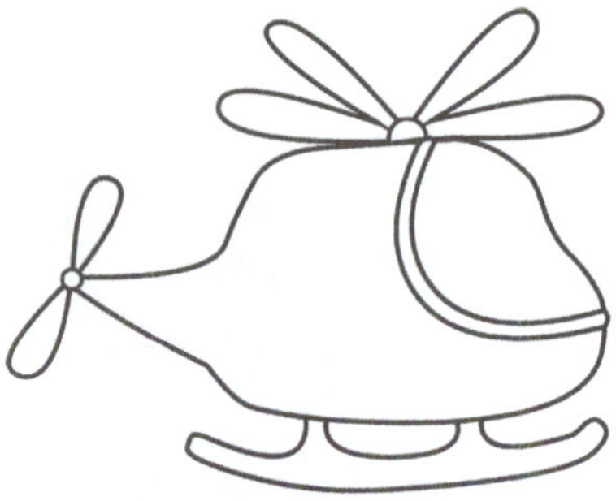

helicopter

elephant

horse

Handwriting

Trace over each letter.

a a a a a

ant

d d d d d

dinosaur

g g g g g

girl

Match the pictures and words. Read them.

hammer

hat

helicopter

house

horse

Add the '**h**' to these words, then trace over the letters.

☐ it ☐ ome ☐ at

Maths

Write how many in each group.

 ☐

 ☐

 ☐

 ☐

Colour the pictures that start with the letter **f**.

f

fish

shirt

fox

face

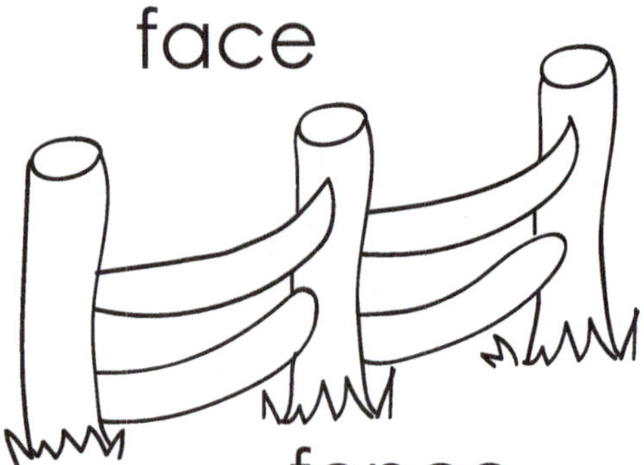

fence

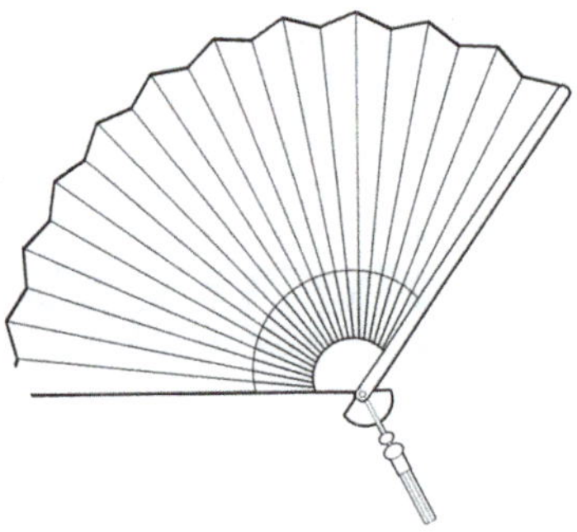

fan

frog

Handwriting

Trace over each letter.

c c c c c

cat

e e e e e

elephant

o o o o o

octopus

Match the pictures and words. Read the words.

fish

frog

fox

face

fence

fan

Maths

Trace over sixes.

6 6 6 6 six six

Colour the group of **six**.

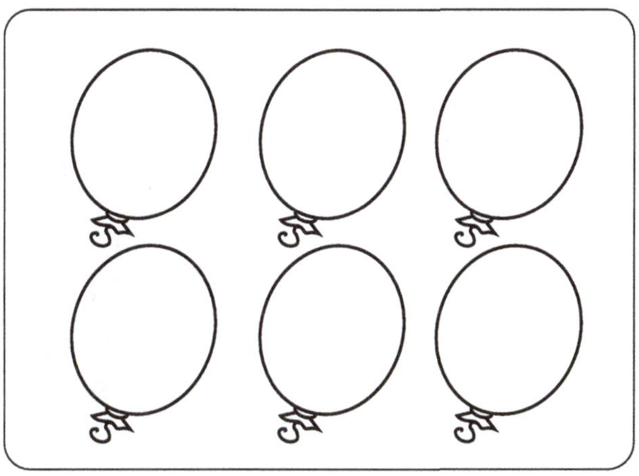
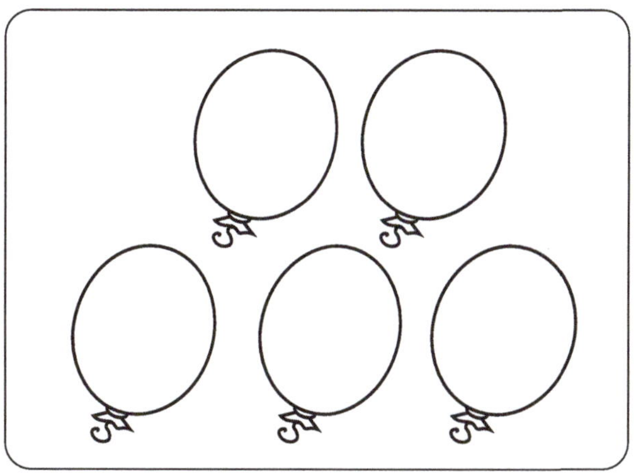

Colour the pictures that start with the letter **g**.

g

goat

girl

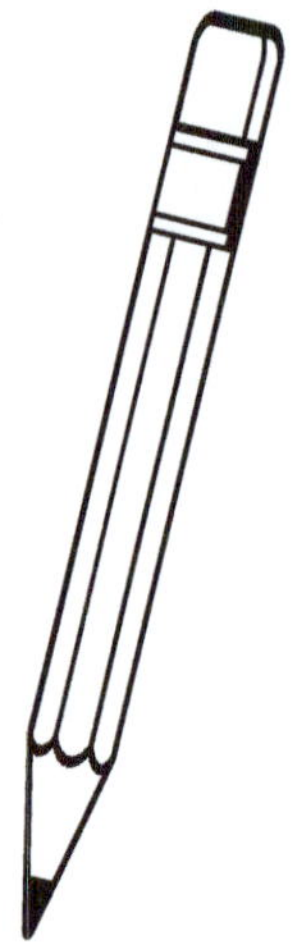

pencil

book

garden

gate

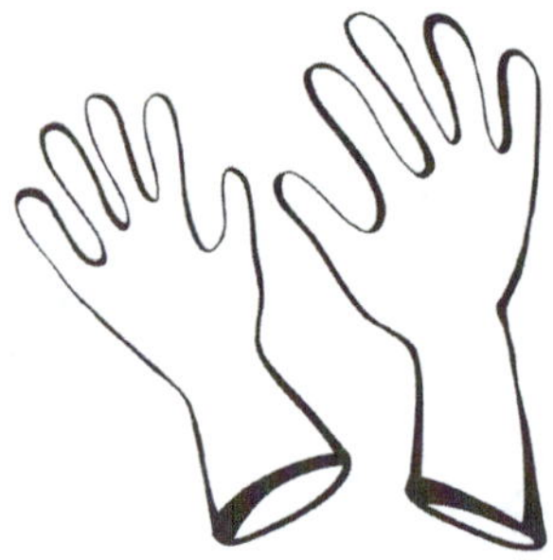

gloves

gun

Handwriting

Trace over each letter.

b b b b b

boy

p p p p p

platypus

k k k k k

king

Match the words to the pictures. Read the words.

gloves

gate

girl

gun

goat

garden

Maths

Colour **half** of each shape.

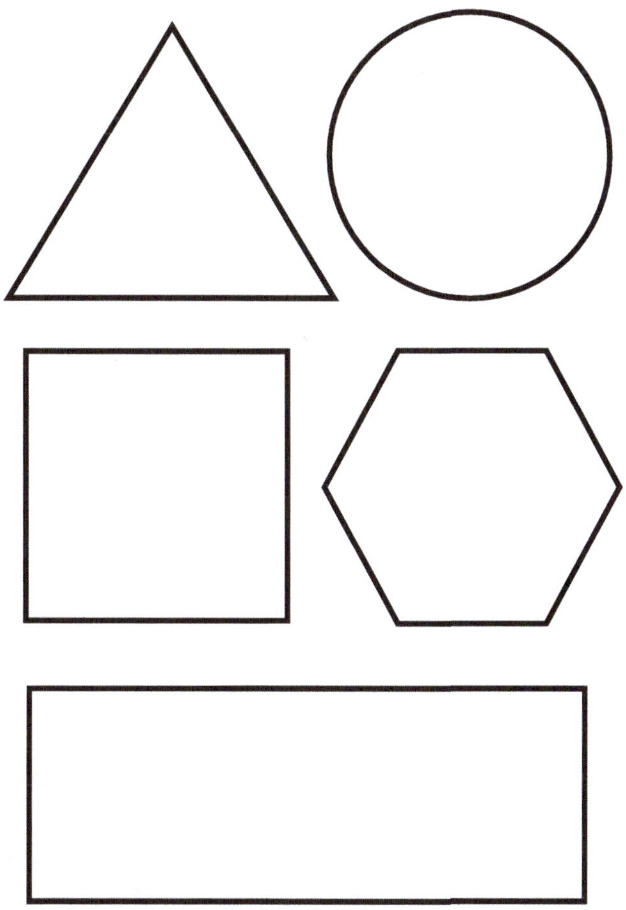

Colour **half** the group of balloons.

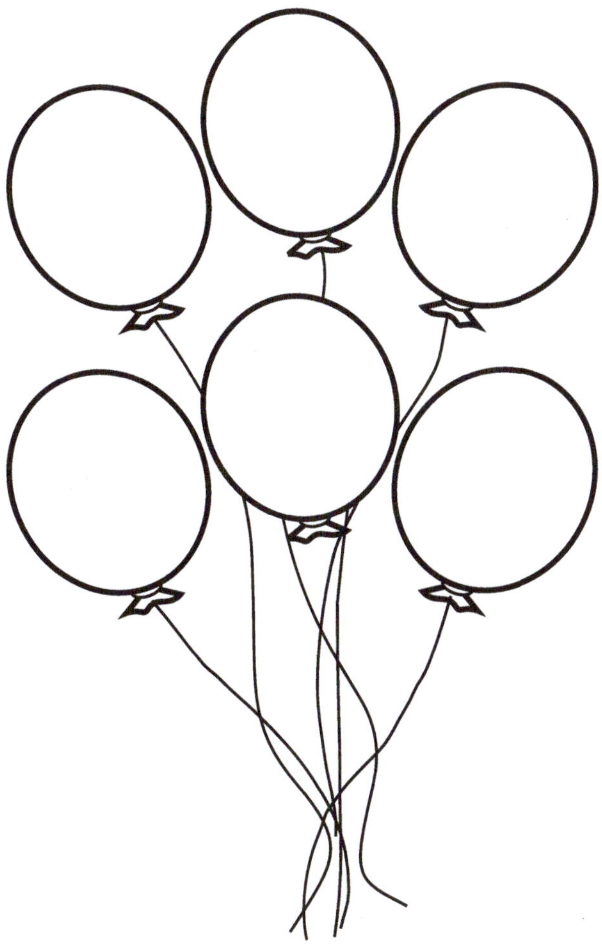

 Colour the pictures that start with the letter **l**.

l

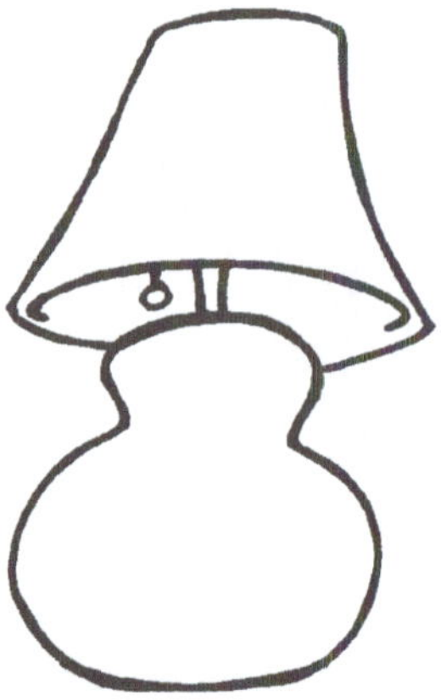

lamp

pig

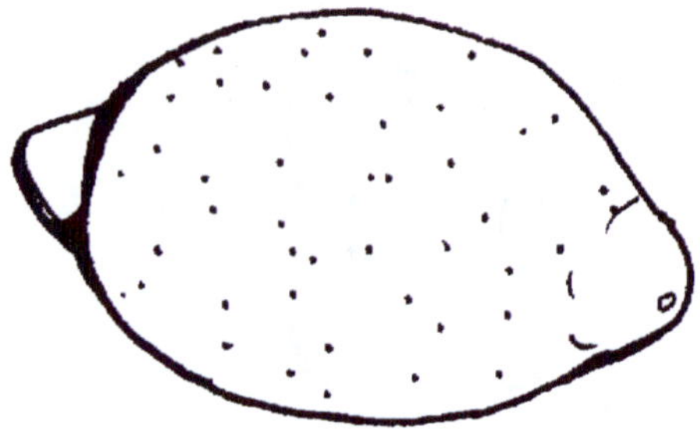

lemon

leaf

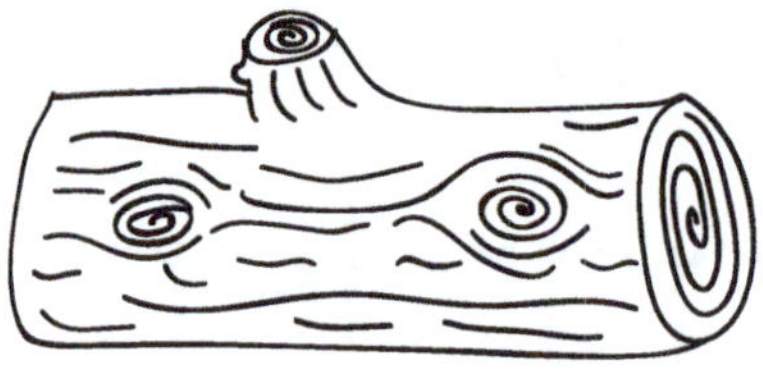

log

lolly

Handwriting

Trace over these letters.

u u u u u u

umbrella

w w w w w

watch

y y y y y y

yo yo

Match the words and pictures. Read the words.

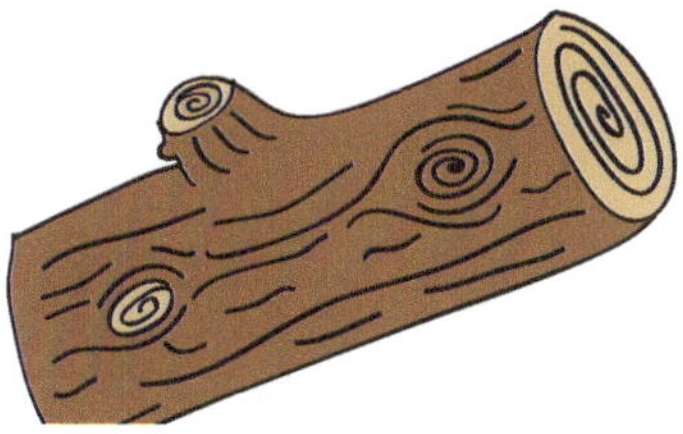
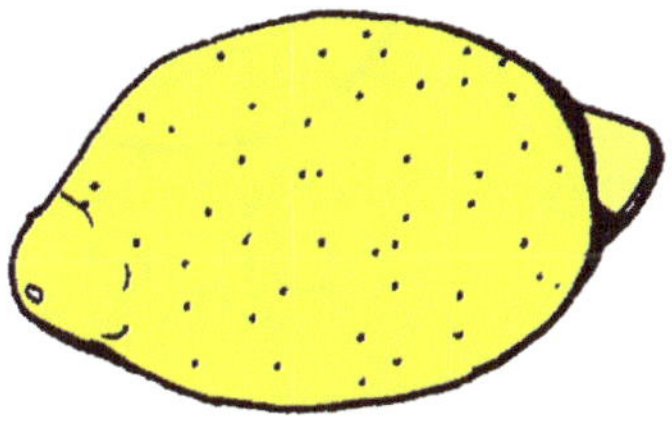

lamp

lemon

leaf

log

lolly

Maths

1. Draw a pencil **shorter** than this one.

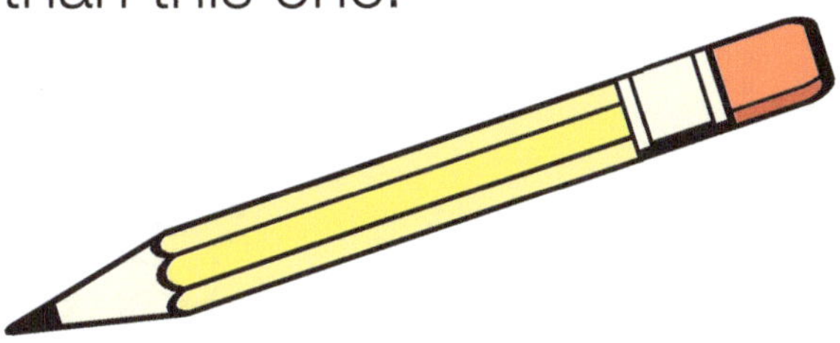

2. Write how many shown on each domino.

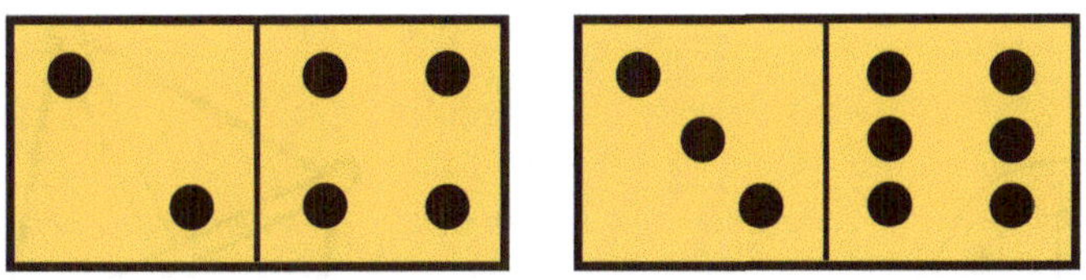

3. Colour the **shorter** log.

4. Count how many stars.

Colour the pictures that start with the letter **p**.

p

pan

cat

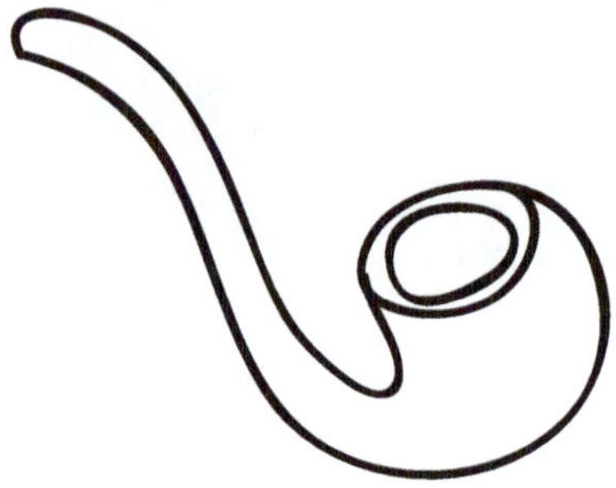

pipe

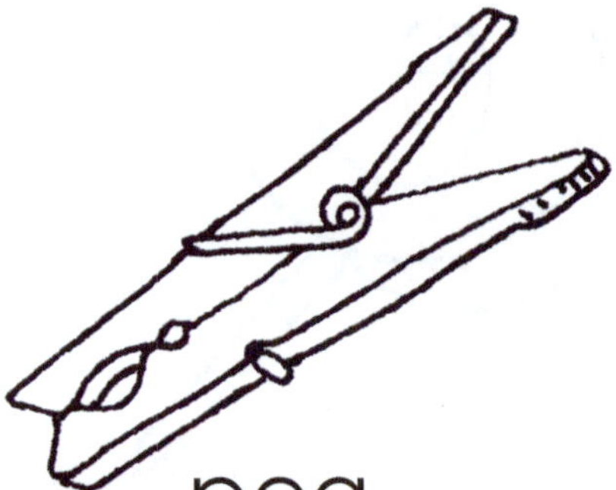

peg

piano

pig

Colour the pictures starting with the letter **j**.

j

jam

jelly

juggler

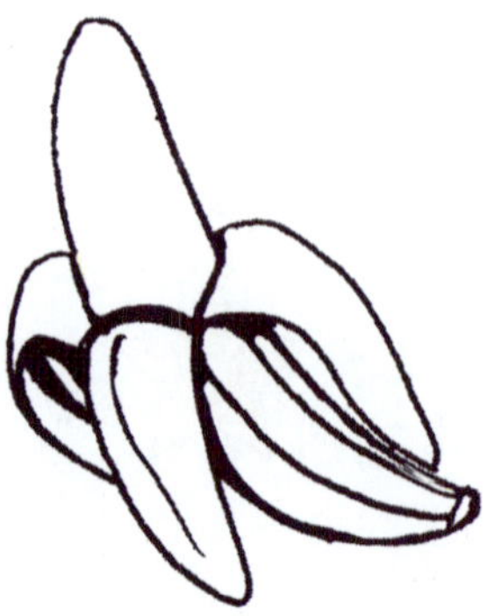

banana

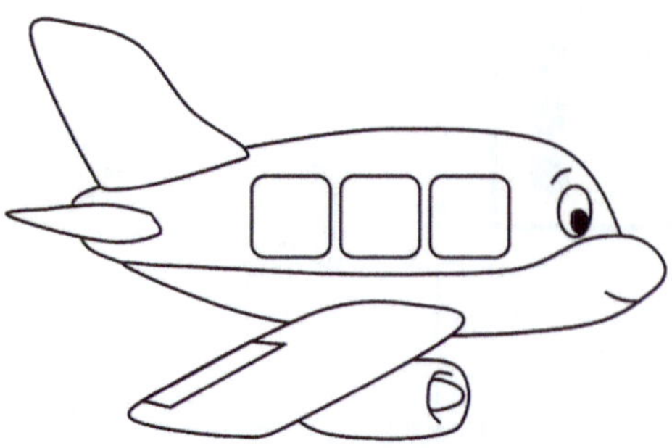

jet

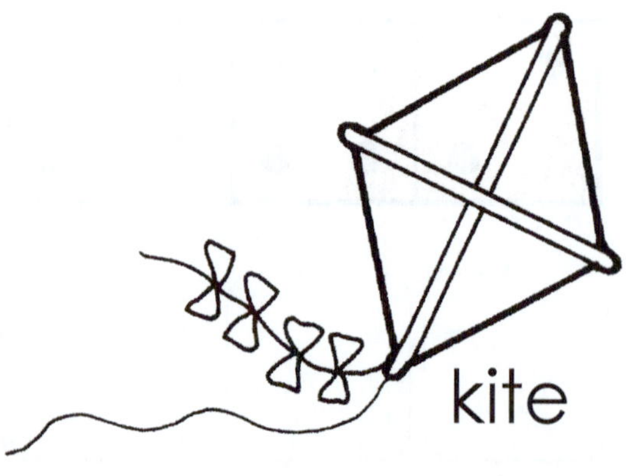

kite

Unit 11 Match the words and pictures. Read the words. Reading

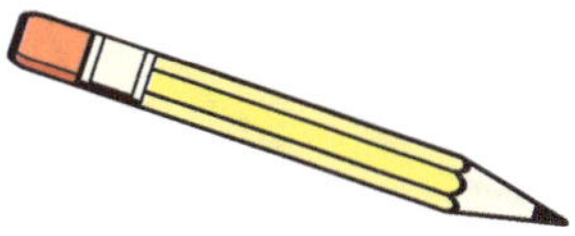

pencil

pig

piano

peg

jet

jam

jelly

juggler

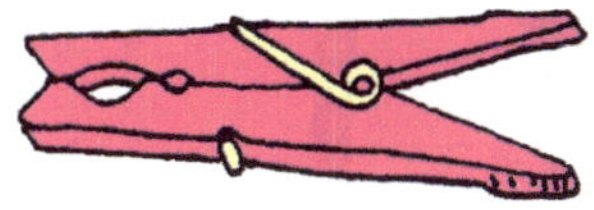

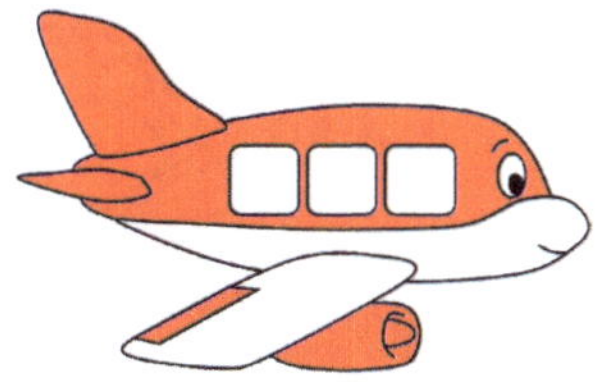

Maths

Trace over the numbers.
Match each number to its group.

7 8 9 10

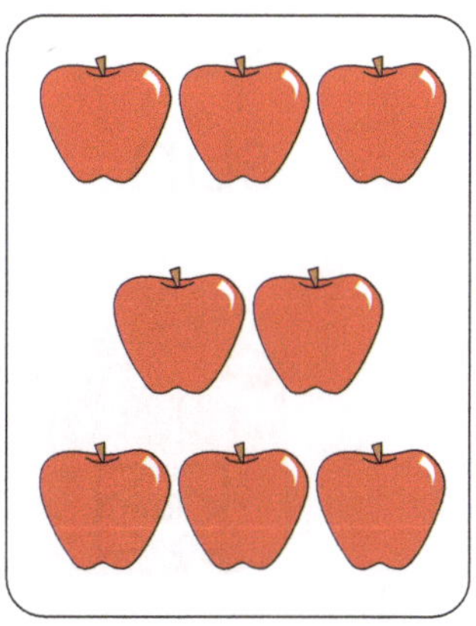

Colour the pictures starting with the letter **n**.

n

nest

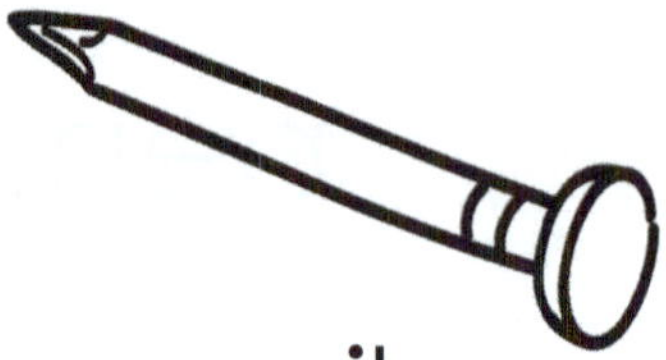

nail

pencil

nose

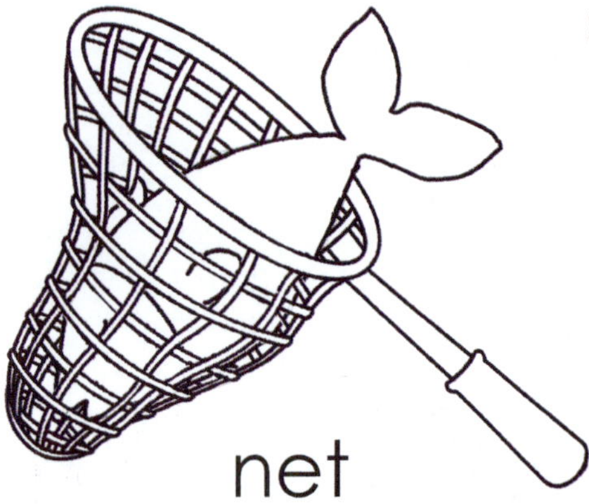

net

nurse

ball

Handwriting

Trace over these letters.

f f f f f f

fox

s s s s s s

sun

j j j j j j

jar

Match the word to its picture. Read the words.

nail

net

nurse

nest

nose

Maths

1. Trace over the word and number zero.

zero 0 0

Draw a fish in the bowl with **zero** in it.

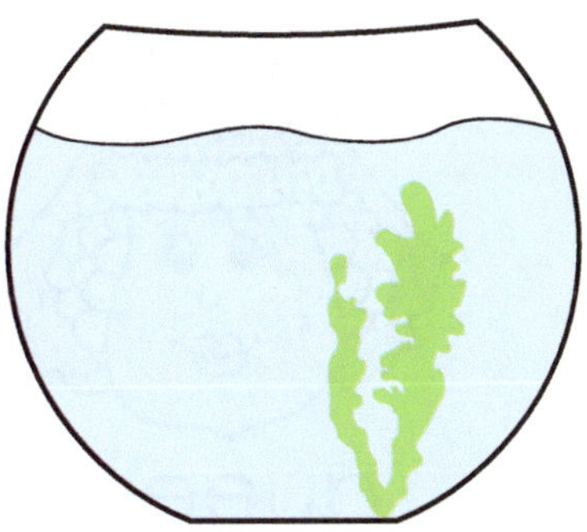

2. Add the missing numbers.

_ 1 2 _ 4

3. Tick the object that would hold the **most**.

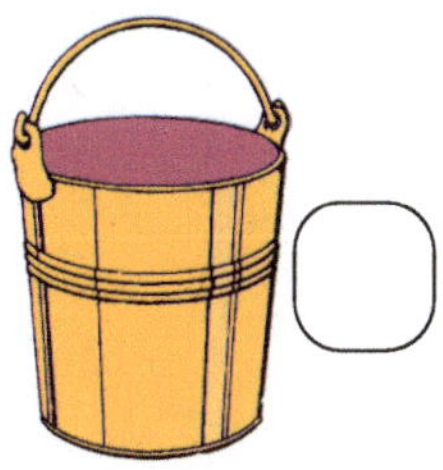
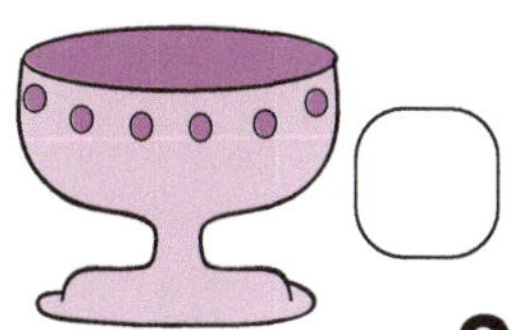

Reading

Unit 13

Colour the pictures that start with the letter **r**.

r

rabbit

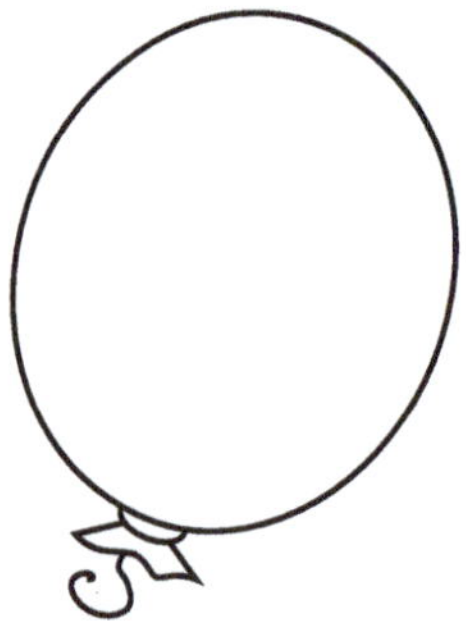

balloon

rug

road

rose

book

Colour the pictures that start with the letter **k**.

k

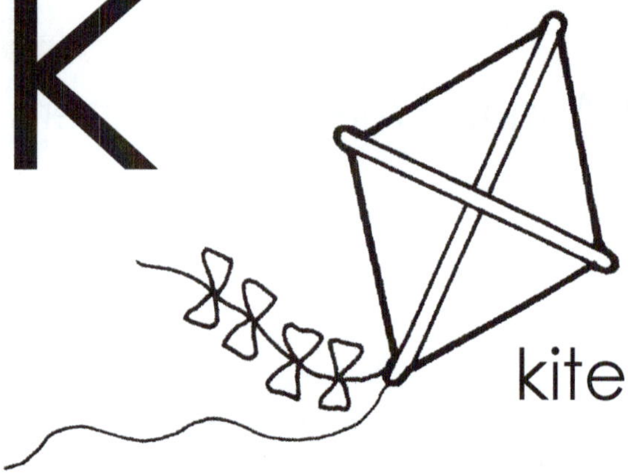

kite

kangaroo

koala

pencil

Handwriting

Trace over these letters.

q q q q q q

queen

Match the word to the picture. Read the words.

rabbit

rug

rose

road

kangaroo

kite

koala

Maths

1. Add these numbers.

2 and 3 make ☐

4 and 2 make ☐

3 and 3 make ☐

5 and 2 make ☐

5 and 4 make ☐

2. Add the missing shapes.

3. Fill in the missing numbers.

1 ___ 3 ___ 5

Colour the pictures that start with the letter **w**.

W

web

hat

wall

watch

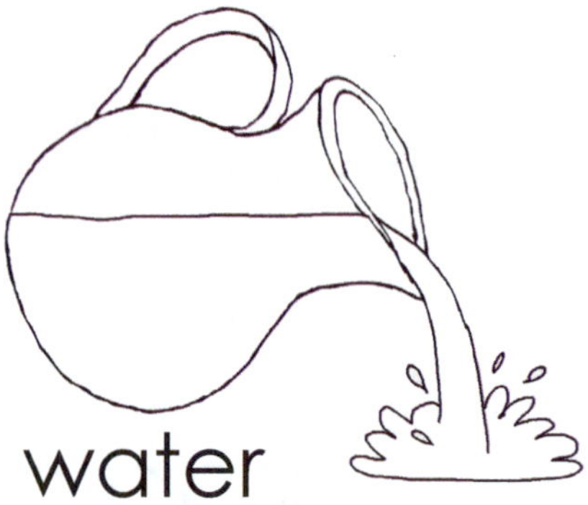

water

witch

Colour the pictures that start with the letter **v**.

V

van

cat

violin

vest

vase

Handwriting

Trace over each letter.

x x x x z z z z

Match the words to the pictures. Read the words.

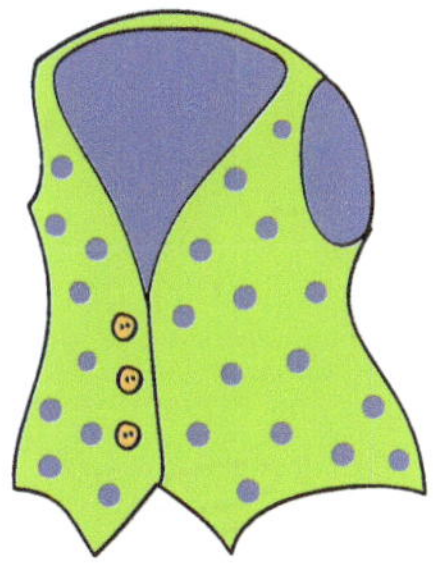

web

wall

water

watch

van

vase

vest

violin

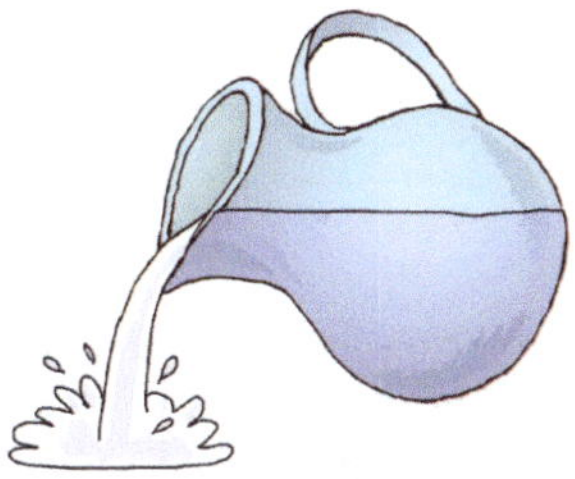

Maths

Match the coloured shapes to the names.

rectangle

square

triangle

circle

Colour the pictures that start with the letter **a**.

a

apple

duck

alligator

angel

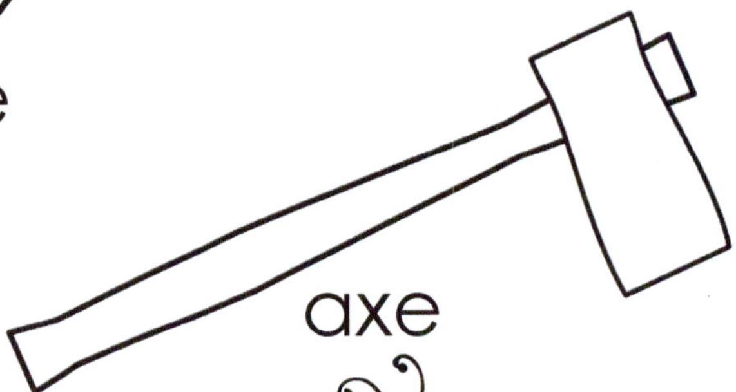

axe

ant

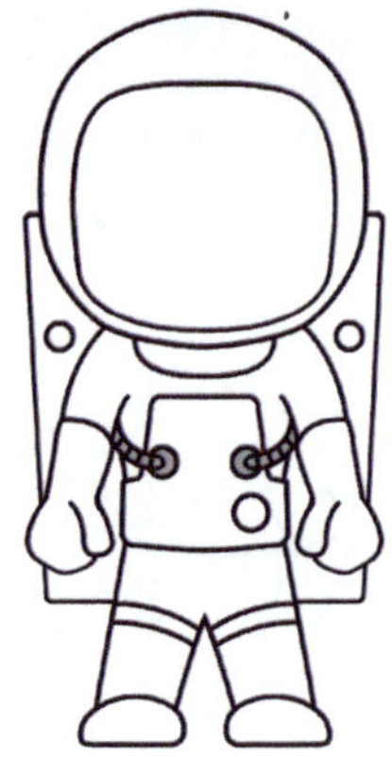

astronaut

Colour the pictures that start with the letter **e**.

e

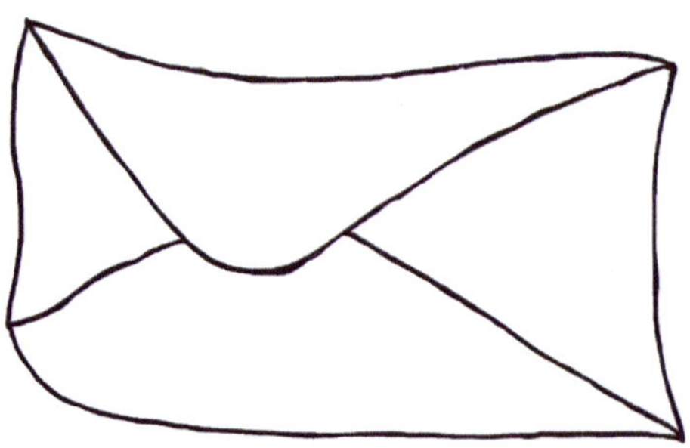

envelope

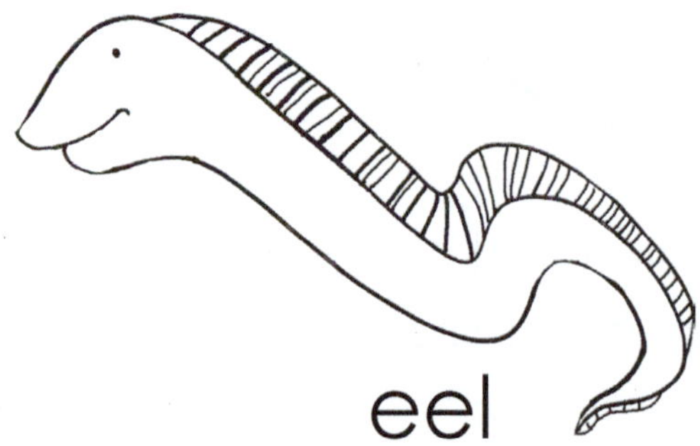

eel

elephant

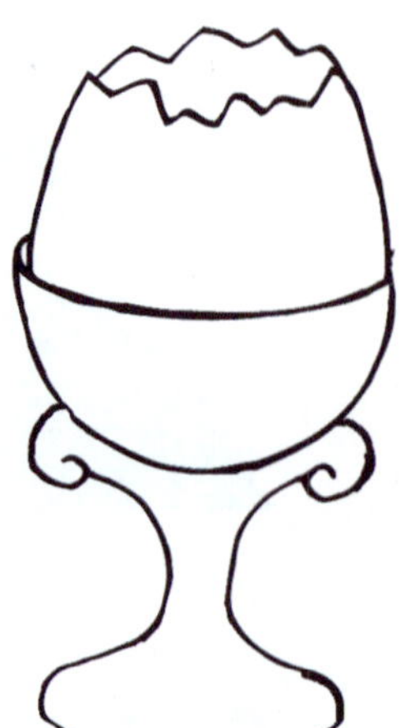

egg cup

jug

van

Unit 15 Match the words to the pictures. Read the words. Reading

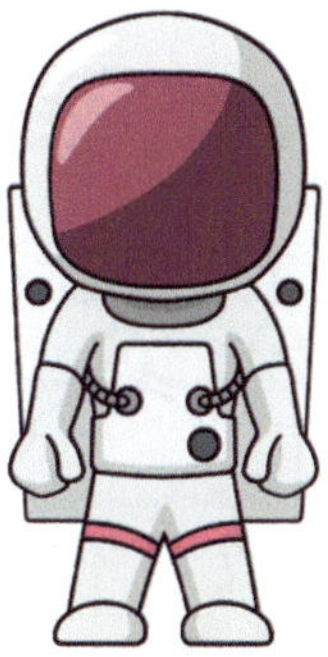

apple

axe

astronaut

ant

alligator

angel

elephant

envelope

egg

eel

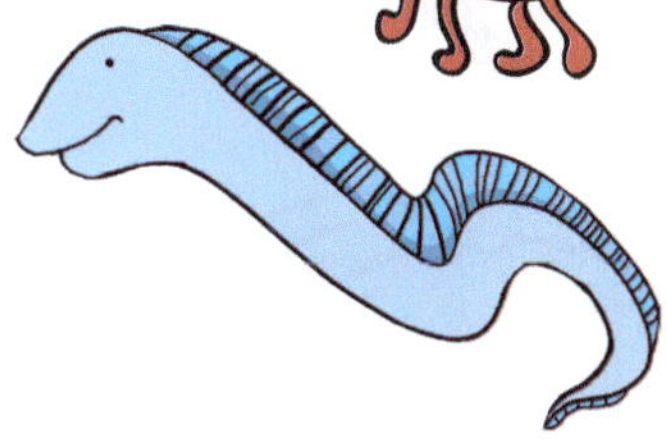

Maths

Colour the **largest** shape in each group.

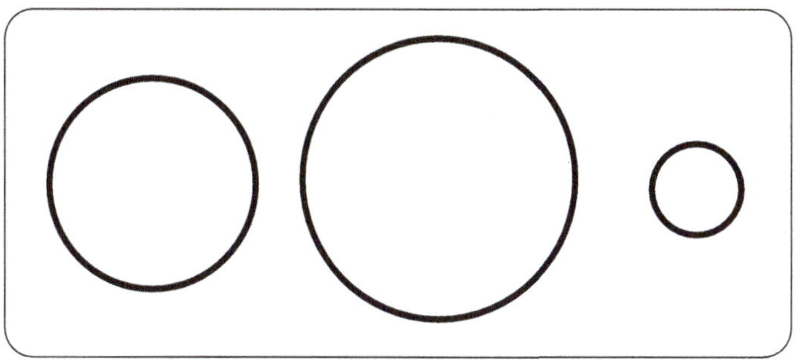

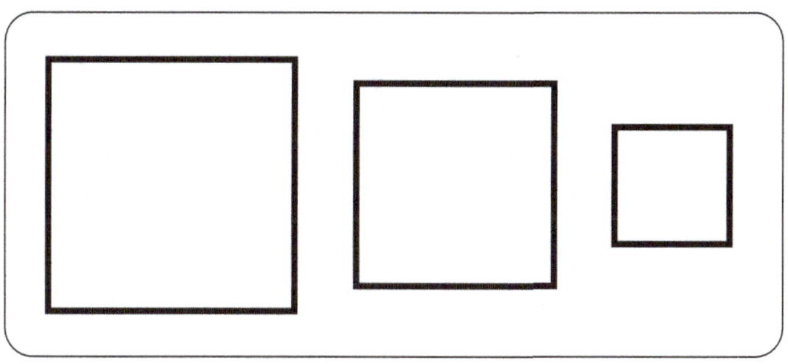
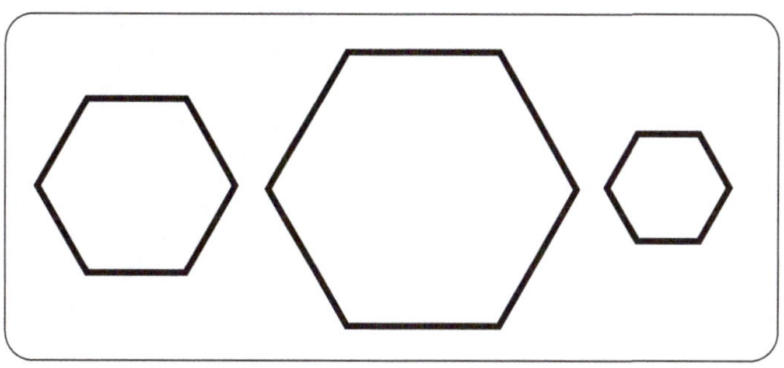

Colour the pictures that start with the letter **i**.

i

apple

igloo

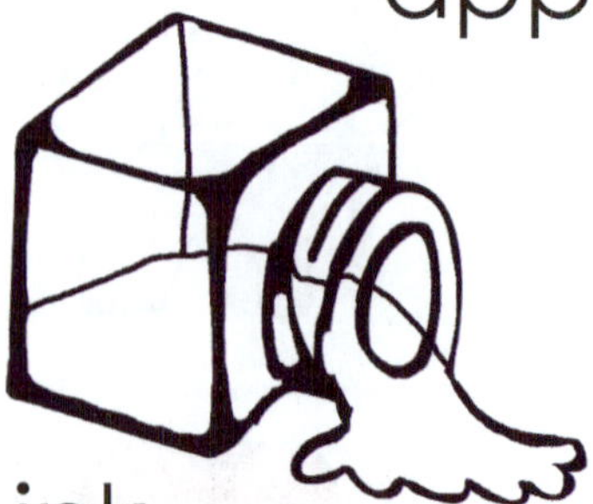

ink

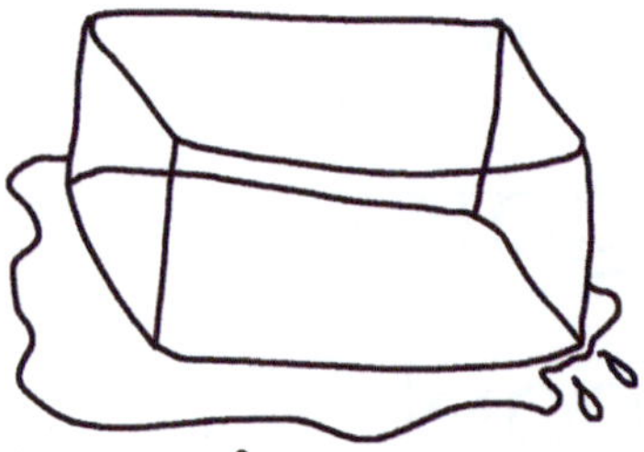

ice

egg

indian

Colour the pictures that start with the letter **o**.

o

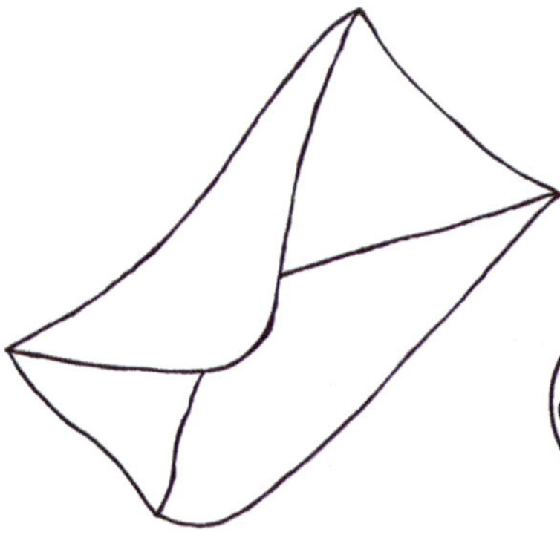

envelope

owl

orange

octopus

Colour the pictures that start with the letter **u**.

u

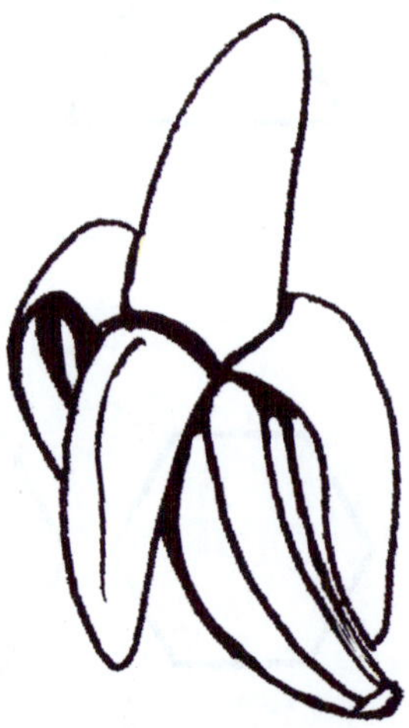

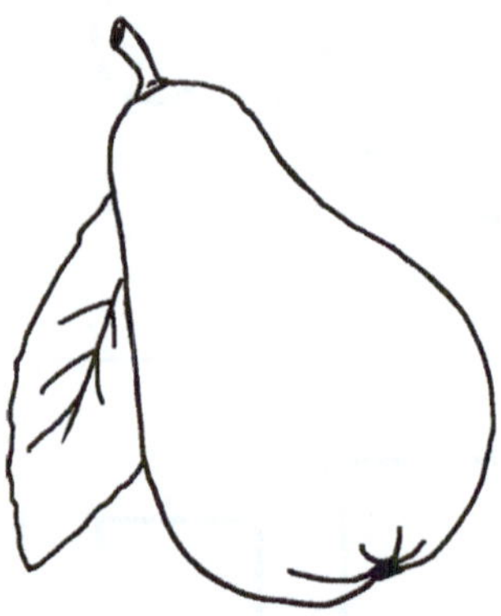

umbrella

pear

ugly

banana

Match the words to the pictures. Read the words.

igloo

ink

ice

indian

orange

octopus

owl

umbrella

ugly

Maths

1. Colour the equal groups using 3 different colours.

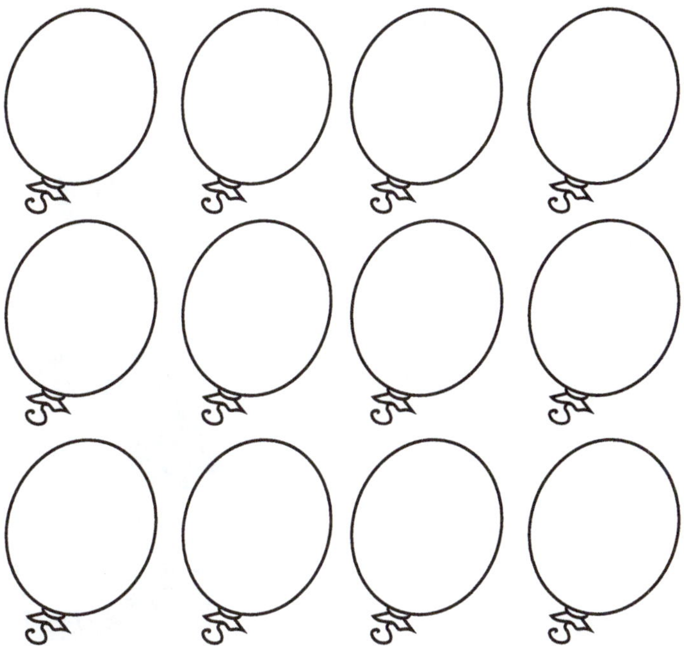

2. Add the numbers on the number line. Fill in the number sentences.

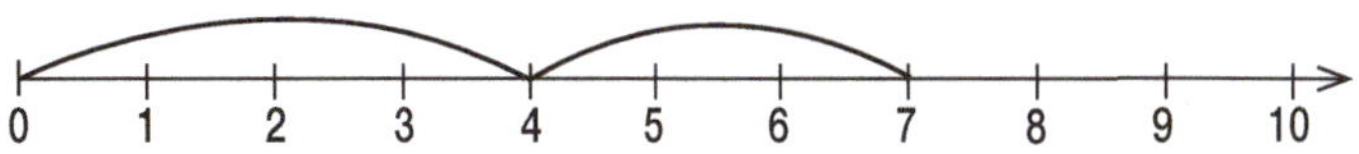

☐ and ☐ make ☐

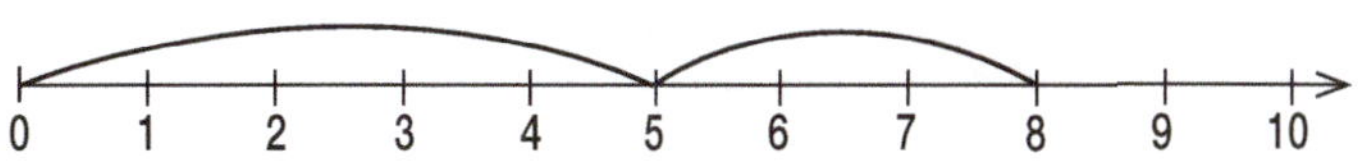

☐ and ☐ make ☐

Trace over the **'at'** words.

at cat rat sat mat

Read the **'at'** poem.

The cat sat on the mat. 

The rat sat on the mat. 

The fat cat sat on the rat. 

Draw a fat cat and a rat.

Match the **'at'** words to the pictures.

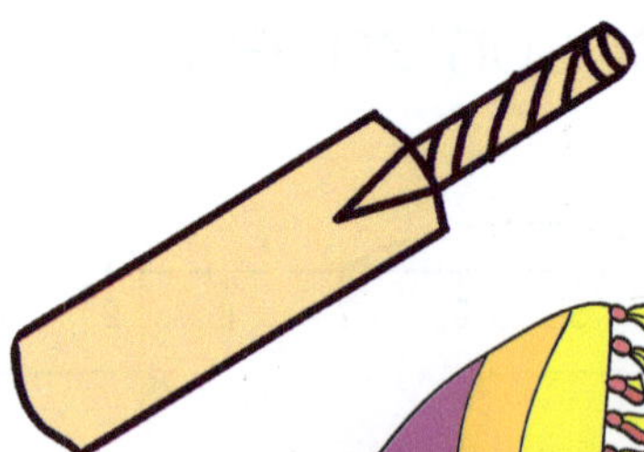

hat

cat

mat

sat

rat

bat

Add letters to the **'at'** sound to label the pictures.

at

at

at

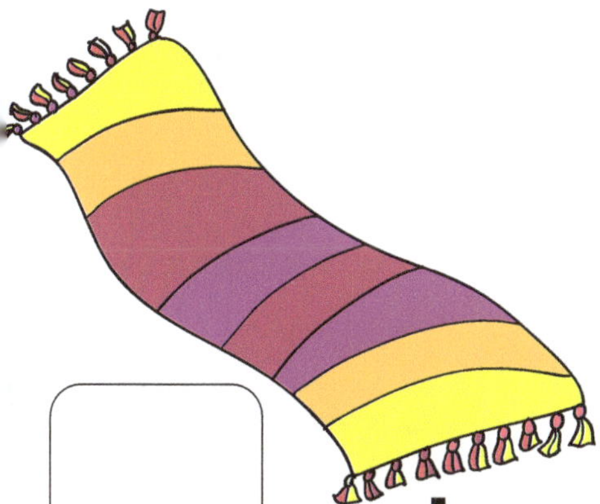

at

at

at

Maths

From the graph:

- Colour the fruit with **the most**.

- Colour the fruit with **the least**.

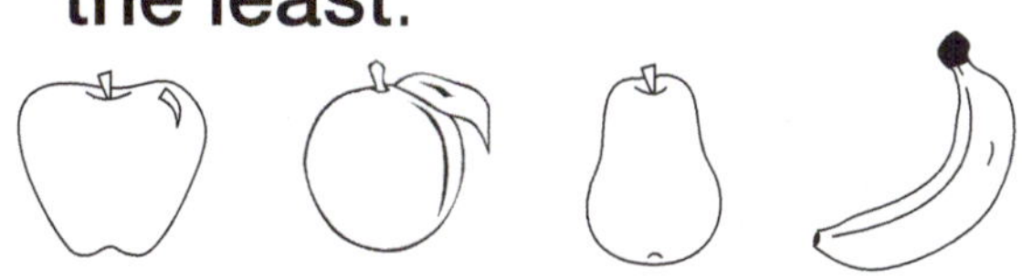

- How much fruit in total?

Reading

Unit 18

Trace over the **'an'** words.

an can man van fan

Read the rhyme.

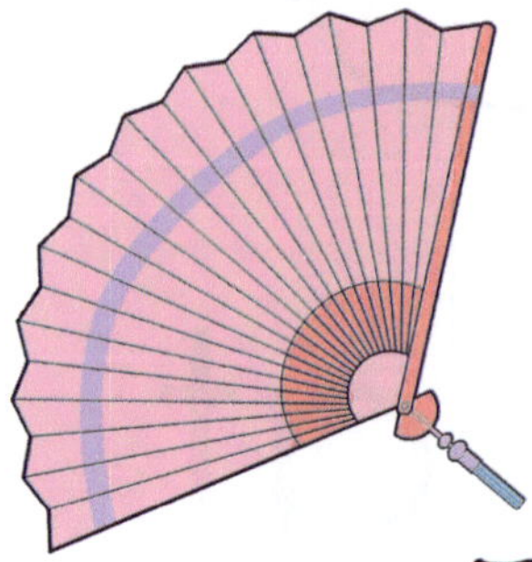

The man in the van
Had a can and a fan.
He ran to the van
With the fan in his hand.

Matching

Match the **'an'** words to the pictures.

fan

can

pan

ran

man

van

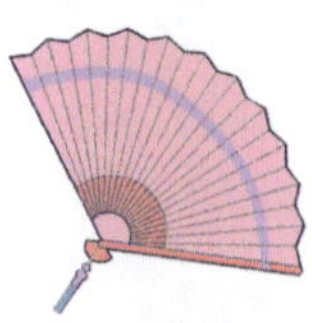

Handwriting

Trace over these capital letters.

A A A A

B B B B

C C C C

D D D D

Add letters to the **'an'** sound to label the pictures.

an

an

an

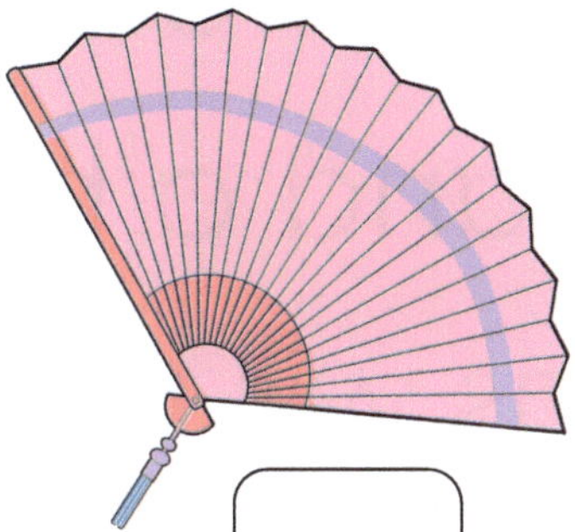

an

an

an

1. Count the number in each group. Write the numbers in the squares.

- 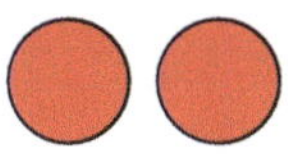 and 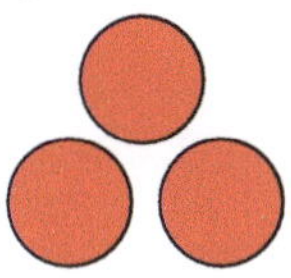 make

  and make

-  and  make

  and make

- 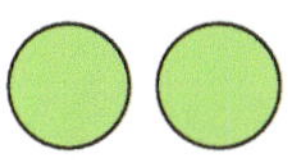 and 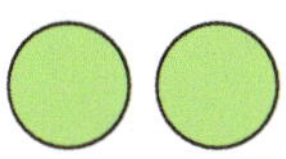 make

  and make

2. Colour everything with 4 legs.

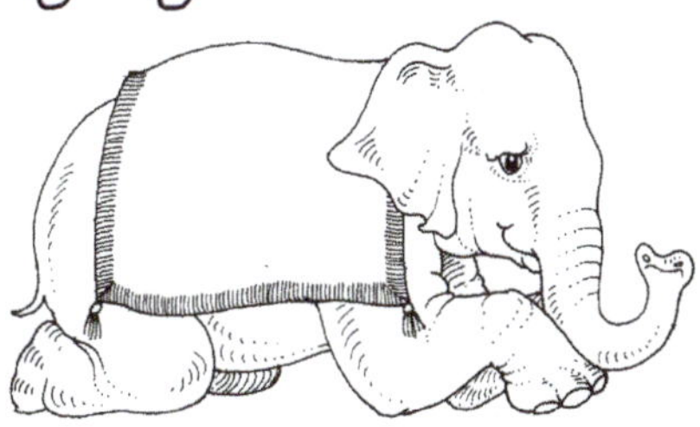

Trace over the words **'un'**.

un bun sun fun run

Read the rhyme.

This fat man sat in sun
He had fun and ate a bun.
He had a fan and a hat
Too many buns will make you fat.

Matching

Match the **'un'** words to the pictures.

sun

bun

run

fun

gun

Handwriting

Trace over these capital letters.

E E E E

F F F F

G G G G

H H H H

Spelling

Add letters to the sounds to label each picture.

☐un ☐un ☐un ☐at

Maths

1. Colour the object that would take **the longest time** to fill.

2. Colour the **lightest** object.

3. Add numbers on the number line. Fill in the number sentence.

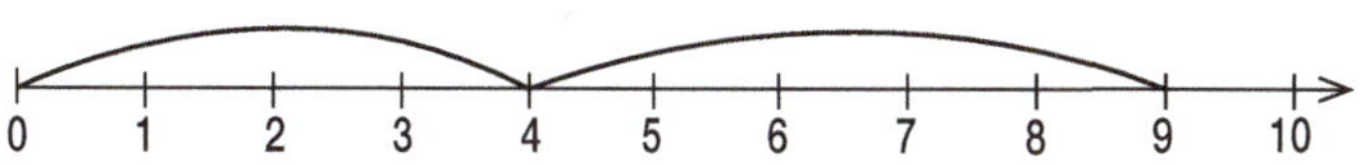

☐ and ☐ make ☐

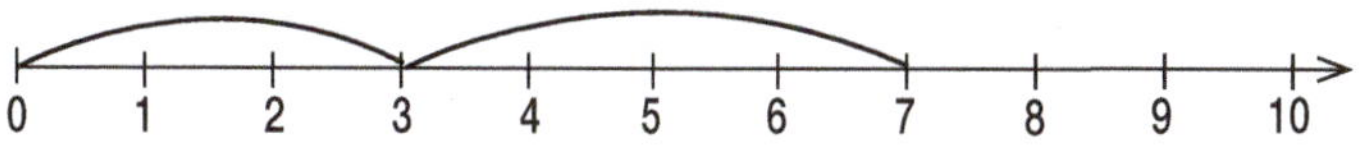

☐ and ☐ make ☐

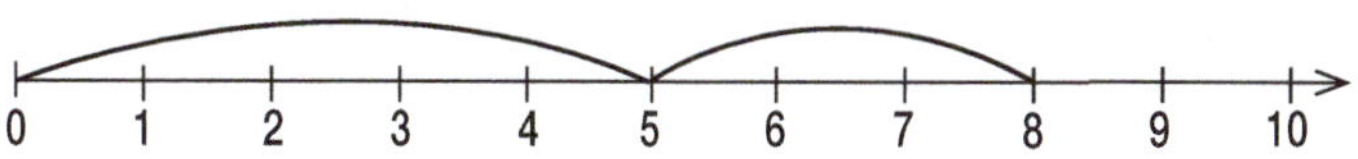

☐ and ☐ make ☐

Trace over the words with each sound.

it bit sit fit hit

ig big pig fig wig

in bin fin pin tin

ot hot lot pot dot

Reading

Read the rhyme.

Look at the pig
It likes to dig.
The baby sits in a cot
Mum puts on her wig a lot.
Look at this pot.
It is very hot.

Add letters to the sounds to label each picture.

☐ ig

☐ ig

☐ in

☐ ig

☐ ot

☐ in

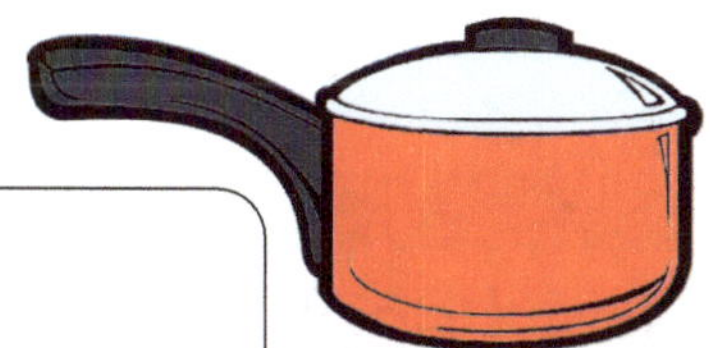

☐ ot

☐ in

☐ ot

Maths

1. Trace over the numbers, then match each one to its name in words.

11	twelve
12	fourteen
13	eleven
14	thirteen

2. Count backwards on the number line to take away. Write each sentence.

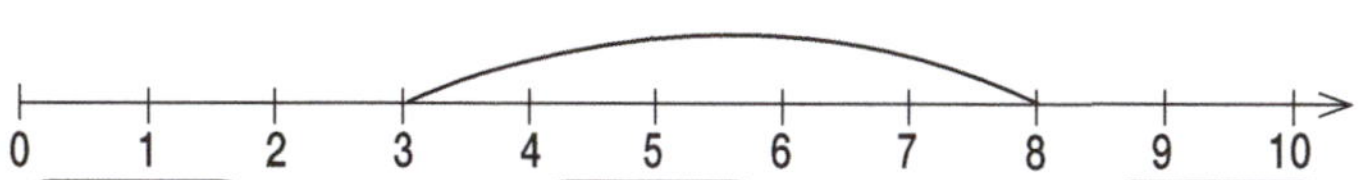

☐ take away ☐ leaves ☐

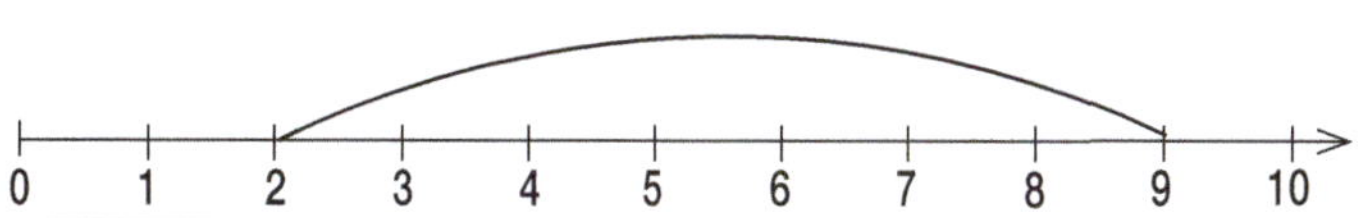

☐ take away ☐ leaves ☐

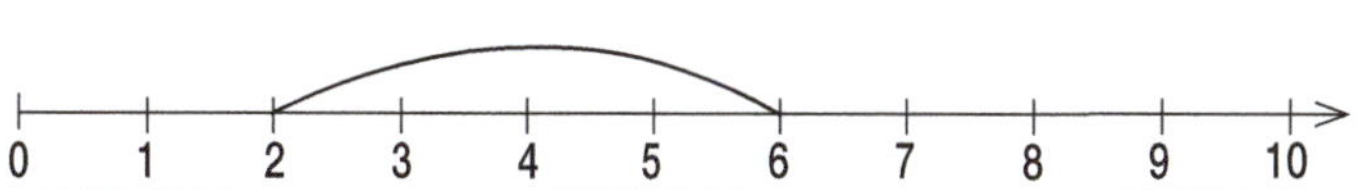

☐ take away ☐ leaves ☐

Read each sentence, then tick what you have at home.

I have a dog at home. ☐

I have a cat at home. ☐

I have a fish in a bowl at home. ☐

I have a sister at home. ☐

I have a brother at home. ☐

Read each sentence. Write your name.

I am a girl. My name is:

I am a boy. My name is:

Handwriting

Trace over each letter.

I I I I I J J J J J

K K K K K L L L L L

Add letters to the sounds to label each picture.

☐og

☐ish

☐rother

☐ister

☐at

☐ome

Maths

1. Trace over the numbers, then match each to its word name.

15	seventeen
16	fifteen
17	eighteen
18	sixteen

2. Colour half of each shape.

Read what I like to do at school.

At school I like to read books.

At school I like to play games.

At school I like to paint.

At school I like to sing and dance.

At school I like to write and draw.

Match the words and pictures.

read

play

paint

draw

sing

Handwriting

Trace over each capital letter.

M M M M N N N N

O O O O P P P P

1. Draw straws.

alongside | above | in front | inside | behind

2. Draw 2 fish **inside** the bowl.

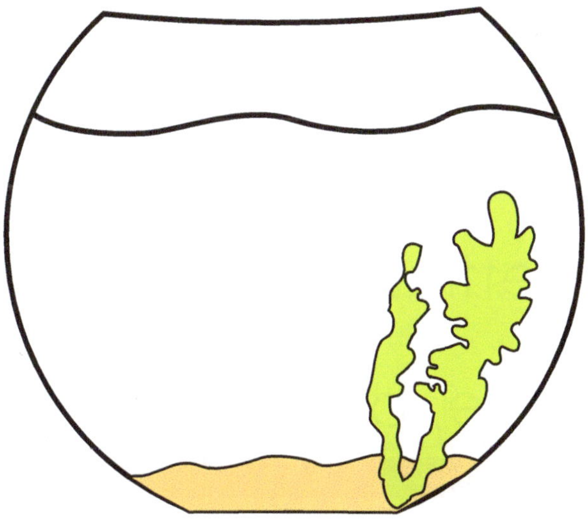

3. Colour the **right hand** glove.

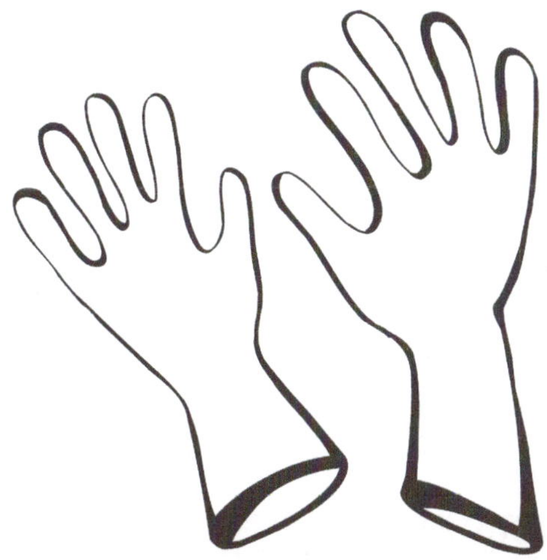

4. Colour the **nearest** tree.

5. Colour the arrows pointing **left.**

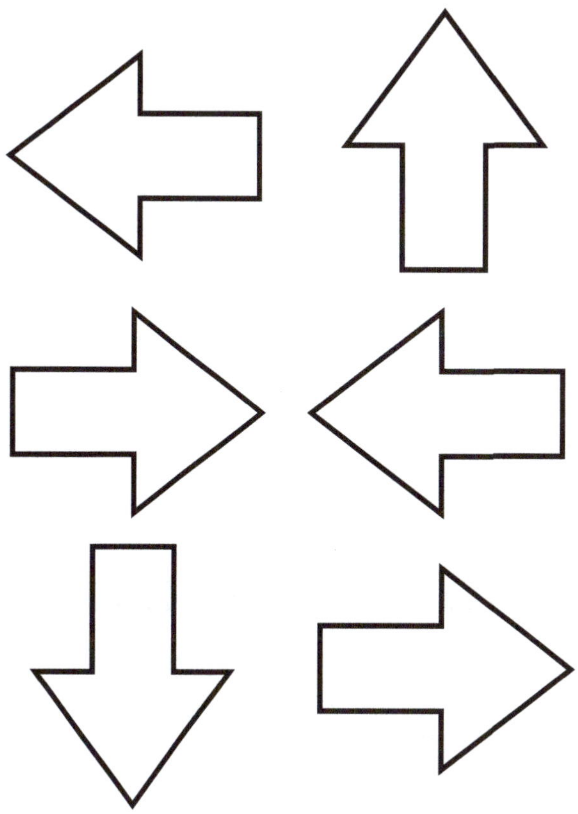

Reading

Read the sentences, then colour the pictures to match.

We have a big red car.

Our house is painted blue.

I have a green bicycle.

My sister has a pink bike.

My brother has a little yellow bike.

All the balloons were orange.

Mum has a black kettle.

I like the colour purple, best.

Comprehension

Complete each sentence by writing the colour.

My bike is _____.

Our house is painted ____.

The balloons were all ______.

Our car is ___.

My favourite colour is ______.

The kettle is _____.

Add letters to label each colour.

☐urple

☐ed

☐ellow

☐lue

☐range

☐reen

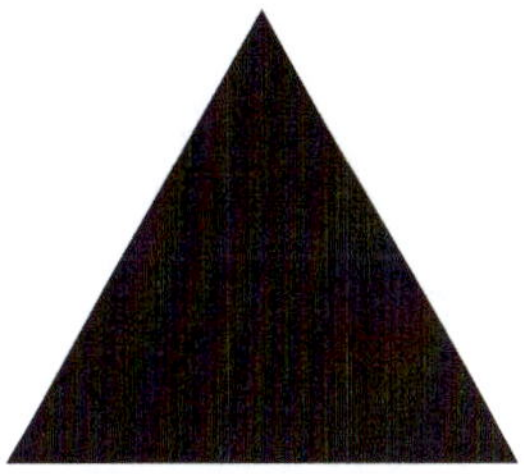

☐lack

☐ink

Maths

1. Match each 3D shape to its name.

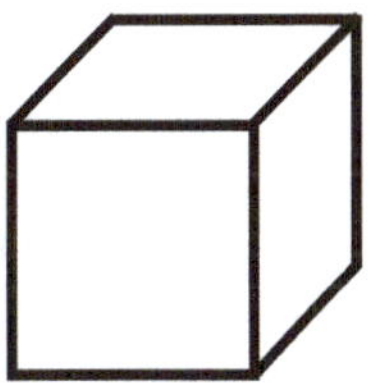

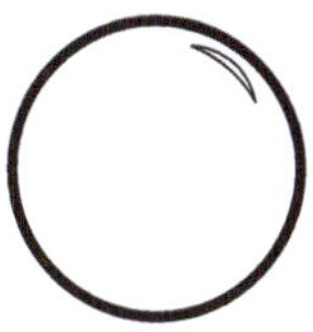

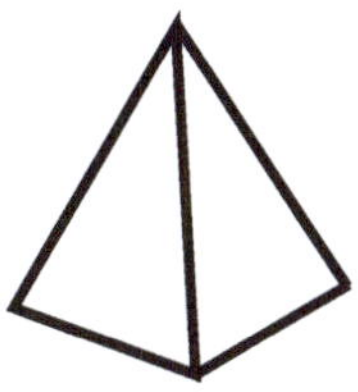

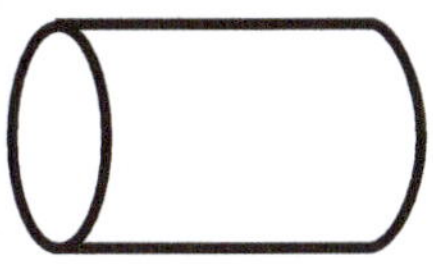

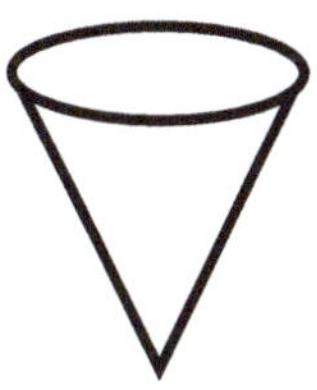

pyramid

cone

cylinder

sphere

cube

2. Add these numbers.

5 and 3 make ☐

7 and 2 make ☐

3 and 4 make ☐

4 and 5 make ☐

6 and 1 make ☐

2 and 4 make ☐

Read the rhyme.

Mum put the tin in the bin.

She fixed her dress with a pin.

Dad put the van in the sun.

We all ran to have some fun.

Help build a sentence.

Mum fixed the dress with a → pin. / bin.

Dad put the van in the → sun. / bin.

Handwriting

Trace over each capital letter, then trace over the words. Copy each word below.

Q Q Q Q R R R R

S S S S T T T T

Queen Rabbit Sun Tie

Add letters to the sounds to label each picture.

☐ in

☐ ress

☐ an

☐ in

☐ in

☐ un

☐ an

Maths

1. Say the days of the week.

Sunday Monday

Tuesday Wednesday

Thursday Friday

Saturday

- How many days in a week? ☐
- What day comes after Sunday?

  ....

- What day comes before Friday?

  ....

- How many school days in a week? ☐

2. Complete these subtractions.

7 take away 4 leaves ☐

8 take away 3 leaves ☐

10 take away 5 leaves ☐

9 take away 2 leaves ☐

6 take away 3 leaves ☐

8 take away 6 leaves ☐

Reading

Read the rhyme.

He used a bat to hit the ball.

The candle was lit in the hall.

The boy and girl want to sit

But he was too fat and would not fit.

- What did the boy hit with a bat? ☐☐☐☐
- Who was with the girl? ☐☐☐
- Who was too fat? ☐☐☐

Punctuation

Add capital letters and full stops.

☐his is a boy○

☐e is six○

☐ur family live in house○

Handwriting

Trace over each capital letter.

U U U U V V V V

W W W W X X X X

Add letters to the words to label each picture.

all

it

all

oy

irl

it

all

Maths

1. 19 nineteen 20 twenty

2. Colour the **first** rosette blue, the **second** red, the **fourth** yellow and the **sixth** green.

3. Fill in the missing shapes in the pattern.

Trace over these words.

day night morning

afternoon today birds

Read the rhyme.

Morning, night, afternoon

Are times we see the sun and moon.

Today is sunny, I hear birds sing.

It is getting warmer, it must be spring.

Tick the best answer.

- The sun comes out at night. ☐ Yes ☐ No
- In spring it is warm. ☐ Yes ☐ No
- Every day has a morning and afternoon. ☐ Yes ☐ No

Punctuation

Add capital letters and full stops.

☐ ornings start a new day ○

☐ oday is warm and sunny ○

☐ fternoons are time to play ○

Spelling

Match each word to the picture it fits best. Discuss.

day

night

morning

afternoon

yesterday

tomorrow

Maths

1. Draw the little hand on each clock.

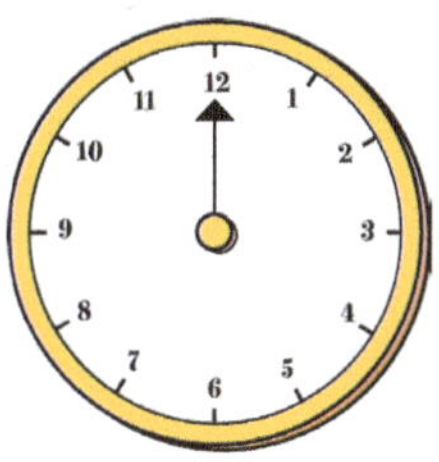
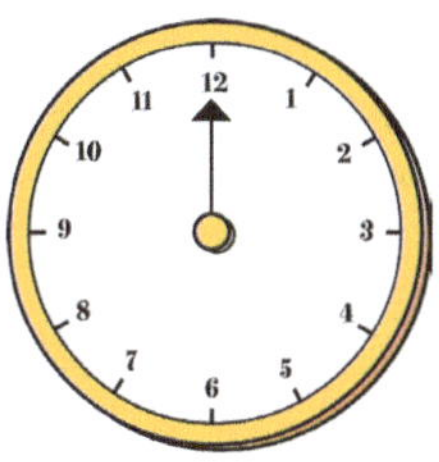
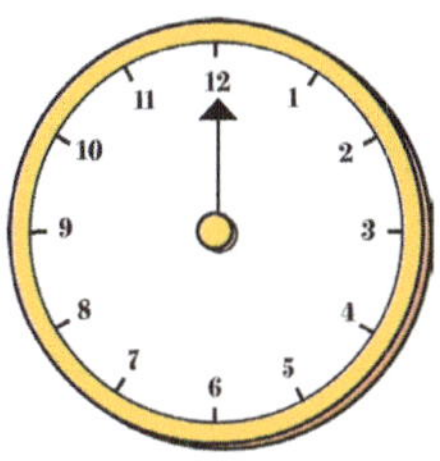

3 o'clock 7 o'clock 10 o'clock

2. Write these as digital time.

6 o'clock

2 o'clock

11 o'clock

8 o'clock

3. Draw a line from each object to its shadow.

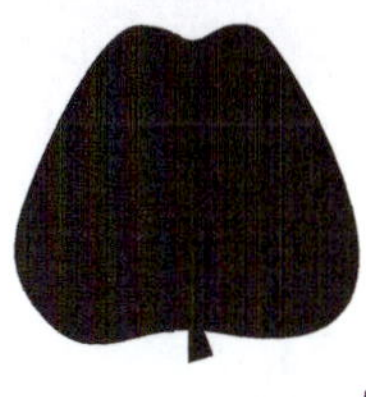

Reading

Read the rhyme.

The boy likes to eat his egg.
He liked it soft and runny.
He ate it slowly with a spoon.
And on his toast he liked honey.

Complete each story path.

The boy ate his egg with a → spoon. / fork.

egg. / honey. ← On his toast he liked

Punctuation

Add capital letters and full stops or a question mark. (?)

☐ ggs on toast are good at breakfast ○

☐ oney is good on toast ○

☐ like my eggs soft and runny ○

☐ o you like honey on your toast ☐

Handwriting

Trace over these capital letters.

Y Y Y Y Z Z Z Z

Add the starting letter to make words from the rhyme.

__gg __poon __oney __iked __oast

__he __is __oft __lowly

Maths

1. Trace over the shape. Draw a line to its name.

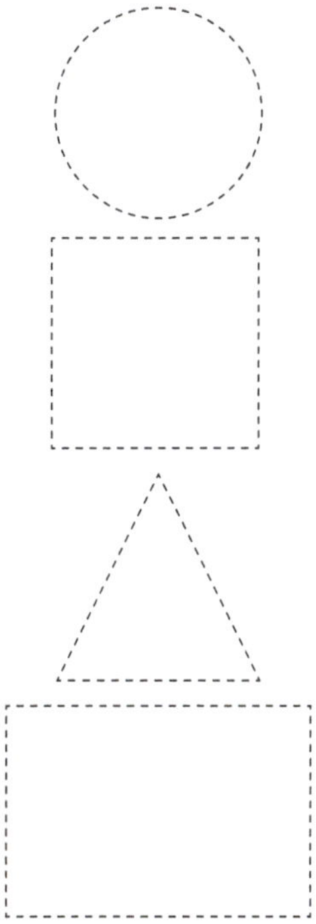

square

triangle

rectangle

circle

2. Colour triangles yellow, squares red and circles blue.

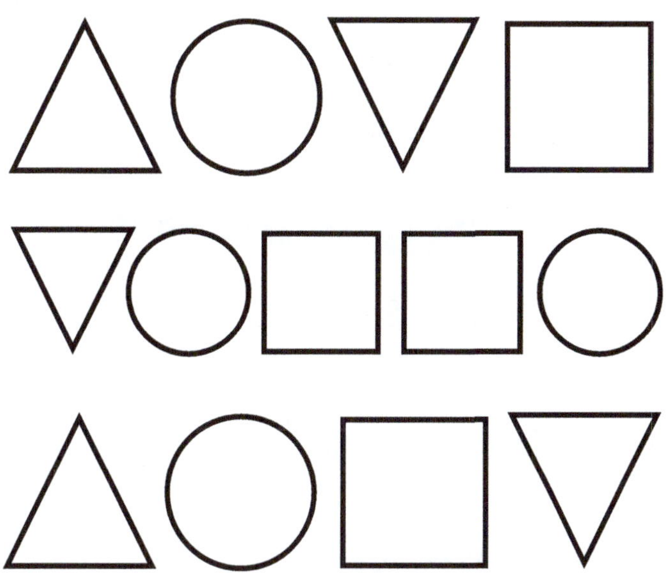

3. Sort the fruit and ice cream. Colour a square for each one to make a graph.

Which is the **most** popular?

____

Which is the **least** popular?

____

Reading

Read the rhyme.

There is a little baby in our house.
When it's asleep we are quiet as a mouse.
Sometimes it cries when it's in bed.
But goes to sleep when it's been fed.

Complete each story path.

The baby at our house is → big. / little.

After the baby is fed it → cries. / sleeps.

We are quiet like a → mouse. / duck.

Punctuation

Add capital letters and full stops or a question mark. (?)

☐abies like to sleep a lot ○

☐he house is quiet when a baby sleeps ○

☐o you go to sleep when you are fed☐

☐re there any babies at your house☐

Money

1. Draw a line from a coin to its name.

twenty cents

one dollar

fifty cents

two dollars

ten cents

five cents

2. Write each total amount.

3. Tick the number of kangaroos on a $1 coin.

4 ◯ 6 ◯ 3 ◯ 5 ◯

4. Which coin has a lyrebird on its face?

10 cents ◯ 20 cents ◯ 5 cents ◯ 50 cents ◯

5. Colour the coins needed to buy each item.

Position

1. Follow the instructions below to plot a path home.

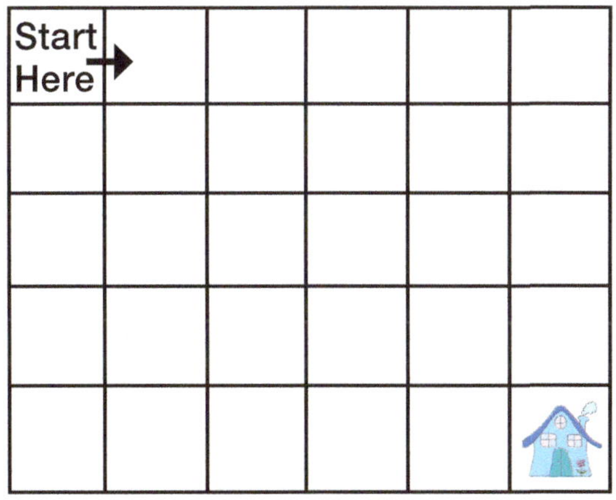

Move straight ahead 4 spaces

Move down 2 spaces

Go left 2 spaces

Go down one space

Go left 2 spaces

Go down 1 space

Go right 5 spaces to home

2. Colour the pair that is **back to back**.

3. Draw a bowl in **front** of the dog and a bone **behind** it.

Read the Nursery rhyme.

Hickory, dickory, dock.
The mouse ran up the clock.
The clock struck one
And down he ran,
Hickory, dickory dock.

Trace over the **ck** words, with the sound of **K**.

ck clock dock rock

duck truck back

Maths

1. Use different colours to make four groups of four balloons.

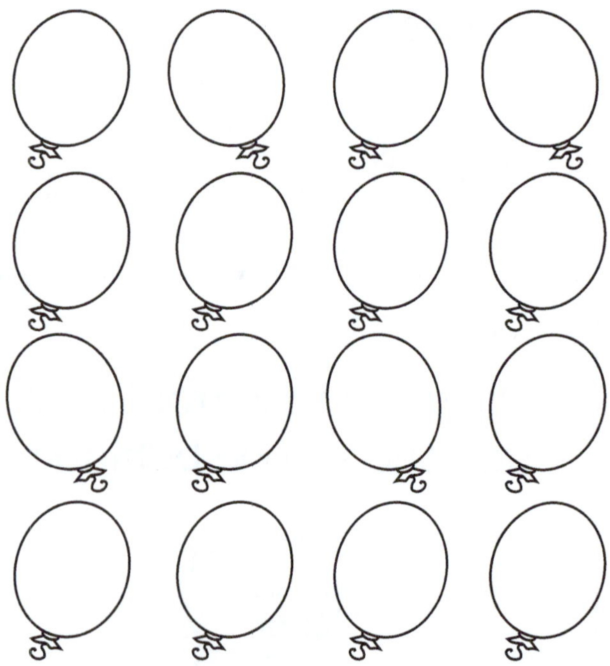

groups of equal

2. Number the containers 1 to 6 **smallest to largest**.

Read what children say.

Complete each sentence.

I always say, ____________________.

I am always, ____________________.

I always wait my ____________________.

Punctuation

Add capital letters and full stops or a question mark. (?)

☐ t is good manners to always say please ○

☐ ut your hand up and wait your turn ○

☐ o you always say thank you ☐

Answers

Unit 1	bus bell boy baby book boy bell bus baby book  one / / / /
Unit 2	man monkey milk mat mum mum monkey mouse man milk mat  two 2 2 2 2
Unit 3	tin tap tie television tea pot tiger tin tap television tiger tie tea pot bottom snake / middle pencil / elephant
Unit 4	scissors snail snake soap six shirt snake six scissors shirt soap snail 1 one 2 two 3 three 4 four 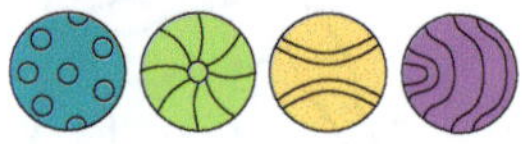
Unit 5	car cow cot cat candle cup cat car cow cup cot candle First bottle / bell
Unit 6	drum dog doll door duck dress dog drum dress doll door duck 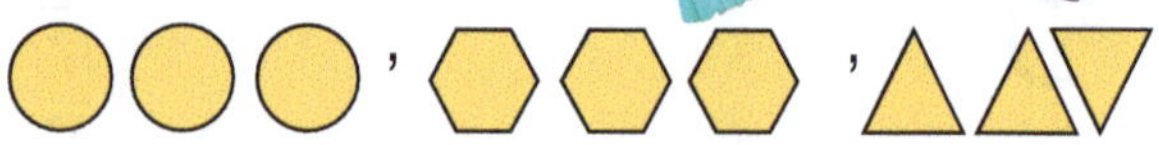
Unit 7	hat hammer house helicopter horse hat hammer helicopter house horse hit home hat / 3 2 1 5
Unit 8	fish fox face fence fan frog fish frog fox face fence fan 6 6 6 six six six / 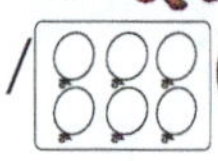 (first group)
Unit 9	gloves girl gate garden goat gun gloves gate girl gun goat garden  / 3 balloons
Unit 10	lamp lemon leaf log lollie lamp lemon leaf log lolly **1.**  **2.** 2 4 3 6 **3.** bottom log **4.** 8 stars

Answers

Unit 11	pan pipe peg pig piano / jam jelly juggler jet pencil pig piano peg jet jam jelly juggler 7 8 9 10 / 7 pears, 8 apples, 9 bananas, 10 oranges
Unit 12	nest nail nose net nurse nurse nail nest nose net **1.** zero 0 0 / fish in first bowl / **2.** 0 3 / **3.** bucket
Unit 13	rabbit rug road rose / kite kangaroo koala rabbit rug rose road kangaroo kite koala **1.** 5 6 6 7 9 / **2.** □ ○ □ / **3.** 2 4
Unit 14	web wall watch water witch / van violin vest vase web wall water watch van vase vest violin ● circle □ square △ triangle ▭ rectangle
Unit 15	apple alligator angel axe ant astronaut / elephant envelope eel egg cup apple axe astronaut ant alligator angel elephant envelope egg eel / centre ○ right ▽ left □ centre ⬡
Unit 16	igloo indian ice ink / orange octopus owl / umbrella ugly orange indian igloo umbrella octopus owl ugly ink ice / **1.** 3 groups of 4 balloons **2.** 4+3=7 5+3=8
Unit 17	cat rat sat mat bat mat hat cat rat sat bat cat hat bat mat rat sat / banana, pear, 14
Unit 18	can man van fan fan can pan ran man van man van pan can fan ran **1.** (2 and 3 make 5), (3 and 3 make 6), (2 and 2 make 4) **2.** chair elephant cat table
Unit 19	bun sun fun run sun bun run fun gun / sun bun fun hat / **1.** bathtub **2.** leaf **3.** (4 and 5 make 9), (3 and 4 make 7), (5 and 3 make 8)
Unit 20	bit sit fit hit / big pig fig wig / bin fin pin tin / hot lot pot dot / pig wig pin fig cot hot bin fin pot / 11 eleven, 12 twelve, 13 thirteen, 14 fourteen / (8 take away 5 leaves 3), (9 take away 7 leaves 2), (6 take away 4 leaves 2)

Answers

Unit 21	parent / dog fish brother sister cat home **1.** 15 fifteen 16 sixteen 17 seventeen 18 eighteen **2.**
Unit 22	read play paint draw sing **1.** **2.** **3.** **4.** big tree at the front **5.**
Unit 23	green blue orange red purple black purple red yellow blue orange green black pink **1.** cube sphere pyramid cylinder cone **2.** 8, 9, 7, 9, 7, 6
Unit 24	pin sun / dress bin van pin tin sun ran **1.** parent / 7 days / Monday, Thursday / 5 school days **2.** 3, 5, 5, 7, 3, 2
Unit 25	ball boy boy [T] . [H] . [O] . ball lit wall boy girl sit tall **1.** 19 nineteen 20 twenty **2.** first 1st blue, second 2nd red, fourth 4th yellow, sixth 6th green /
Unit 26	day night morning afternoon today birds no yes yes [M] . [T] . [A] . night morning afternoon yesterday tomorrow day **1.** **2.** 6:00 2:00 11:00 8:00 **3.**
Unit 27	spoon honey [E] . [H] . [I] . [D] [?] egg spoon honey liked toast The his soft slowly **1.** circle square triangle rectangle **3.** ■■■ ■■■■ ■■■■■■ ■■■■ orange apple **2.**
Unit 28	little sleeps mouse [B] . [T] . [D] [?] [A] [?] **1.** twenty cents one dollar fifty cents five cents two dollars ten cents **2.** 80 cents, \$1.55 **3.** 5 kangaroos **4.** 10 cents **5.** 50 cents 20 cents 10 cents / \$1 / **1.** parent **2.** first two girls **3.** parent
Unit 29	clock dock rock duck truck back **1.** 4 groups of 4 equals 16 **2.** egg cup 1, soft drink 2, jug 3, bin 4, sulo 5, bath 6
Unit 30	please / good / turn [I] . [P] . [D] [?]